PARAMETERS OF THE SOUL

Toward a Christian Psychology

ROLLIN JAY KIDWELL

ISBN: 0963971832

ISBN 13: 9780963971838

Library of Congress Control Number: 2012918909
CreateSpace, North Charleston, SC

To my family
The blessings of my life
Perpetually at a fork in the road
I pray they choose wisely

PARAMETERS OF THE SOUL

Toward a Christian Psychology

Table of Contents

Introduction

My Bible College education only lasted three semesters before a restless spirit moved me to transfer to a local university in search of a line of study that was a better fit with my gifts and interests in life. After a semester attending classes in the education department, I finally settled in with the psychology folks and earned my Bachelor's degree. It was an enjoyable experience as I studied under professors that appeared to live their lives much as I did. After graduation I applied to a number of graduate schools in psychology and I was fortunate to be accepted to what was then one of the top psychology programs in the country, albeit for only my Master's degree. One evening, as I was walking through the parking lot toward the psychology building where I had an evening class, I ran into one of my former Bible College professors who moonlighted at the university. We engaged in some small talk as we walked toward the campus and just as we were about to part ways he firmly grabbed hold of my shoulder, stopped me, looked directly into my eyes and with sincere concern said, "you be careful Jay. The professors in that building have torpedoed many a Christian." As I continued to class, I pondered his warning. This was the 1980's and an increasing number of academics in professional psychology programs believed that God was only for the weak and needy and that religion was nothing more than a crutch used by people who were not strong enough to survive the real world on their own. I had noticed that most of my graduate professors were antagonistic toward religion in general, however, my personal Christian faith had not really been threatened to that point. I wondered when and how the attack might come?

I actually hit my first snafu due to my own incompetence. I found myself at that point in my graduate program where I was to begin my supervised psychotherapy practicum and I was scheduled to meet with my first client on Thursday evening. I had an undergraduate degree and a number of semesters of graduate work in psychology behind me; yet, I knew I was totally unprepared to do real psychotherapy - I was clueless. I naturally reflected back on the various courses I had taken in an effort to identify any specific learning experiences that would enable me to engage in real psychotherapy. I was at a loss on how to take the theoretical knowledge I had acquired and apply it in a real counseling setting. I visited with a few of my professors, conveyed my apprehension regarding the situation, and asked for additional guidance. Each provided direction, based on their personal, narrowly defined theoretical persuasion, just as they had in the classroom. The disparity of their guidance only bolstered my lack of confidence. I had studied so many theories of psychotherapy; many having some semblance of logic, choosing one theory to apply to any problem I might encounter seemed impossible.

I was relieved when I ran into Marie, who was also scheduled to begin her practicum. I had not had many classes with Marie, however, we discovered early in the program we were both Christians, a rare commonality in the graduate program at the university we were attending, and we commiserated when we could. I communicated my concern to Marie and with a hint of sarcasm in her voice she replied, "So, what you are saying is that you are really troubled by this situation and it is negatively affecting your mental health." It was immediately obvious that Marie not only had the same concerns I had, she had settled in on a solution – she would just "reflect." Reflecting is a counseling technique whereby the counselor mirrors what a client said with the addition of any missing affective content. It can facilitate rapport building and is useful in eliciting feedback from the client to ensure accuracy of understanding, however, reflecting alone is typically not enough to lift a client from a state of despair. The clients we would be seeing would be experiencing real emotional pain that would have to be addressed at a deeper level. I wanted to help - not just reflect. When Thursday evening came to pass and my first three counseling sessions came to an end, I had a feeling of satisfaction with the way the sessions had progressed. I took a moment to contemplate the technique I had used and I discovered - I had reflected! Thankfully, over the course of the next six months I began to figure out this special relationship that I began to affectionately refer to as "the mystique of psychotherapy."

After my practicum was complete and I was putting the final touches on my thesis and anticipating graduation, I found myself in a familiar and comfortable chair in the office of the Dean of the psychology department. The Dean had befriended me during my first semester and we had subsequently spent many enjoyable hours talking about religion, psychology, psychotherapy and his pending retirement. On that last visit I brought up some of the concerns I had as I progressed through the program. I told him about my former Bible College professor's admonition and my assessment that it had not been warranted. I'll never forget what he said to me in response. "Jay," he said as he leaned back in his chair, "This is an arrogant bunch we're dealing with here. I don't think one of them would claim to believe in God, although I personally think there is something reasonable about the belief. In the academic world the professors here are respected for knowing more about the human mind than anyone on this earth. I think we can safely infer, as far as they are concerned, they are as close to being gods as anyone you will ever meet." When I voiced my concerns about not really being taught how to engage in psychotherapy, he replied, "For being gods, you would think they would have some decent answers for the serious questions in life." He then laughed, obviously reading much more into the reply than his words conveyed. Thankfully, I graduated without incident.

I was relieved when I was accepted into a doctoral program that was founded on a humanistic philosophy of learning. Structured from a contradiction, humanism places a high value on value neutrality; the belief that it is inappropriate to place ones personal values on another person, except for the value of value neutrality, of course. So attacking anyone for their religious beliefs, or just about any other beliefs they might have, is unacceptable. While I did not have to worry about any torpedoes bearing down on my faith, I discovered that this value neutral approach broadened the range of acceptable models of psychotherapy. Rather than gaining clarity, I realized I would have to rely on what I had learned through experience as I engaged in the mystique of psychotherapy.

When I began teaching at a Christian university, I quickly discovered I was not capable of explaining the mystique of psychotherapy to my students any better than my professors had explained it to me. This fact really hit home when students, facing an upcoming practicum, came to me seeking more guidance just as I had done when facing my practicum. One thing I was certain of; this was not God's intention as He commanded us to love one-another and promised us that His word was sufficient to equip us to every good work (see 2 Timothy 3:16,17). Consequently, I began to search Scripture in earnest for answers. The primary criticism leveled against the development of a Christian psychotherapy is that the Bible does not specifically address the counseling relationship. That is true, because the Bible is actually a guide for all facilitative relationships of which counseling is only one. The development of a Christian psychology, a Biblical study of the human soul, should provide insights into all Christian facilitative relationships. As I pondered this, I realized the mystique I had attributed to the psychotherapy relationship existed, to a greater or lesser degree, with every relationship I had personally experienced. It is difficult to educate others to be teachers, ministers and parents, yet, teachers, ministers and parents seem to figure out the mystique associated with each relationship over time - some better than others. If God's word is truly sufficient to equip us for every good work, it is sufficient to equip us to be teachers, ministers, elders, parents, neighbors and counselors, all relationships I have come to refer to as "Christian one-anothering." As I began to explore with the broader goal of developing a Christian psychology, rather than a Christian psychotherapy, a pattern began to form that illustrated dynamics of how we personally come into relationship with God through Jesus Christ, then, facilitate on behalf of Jesus as we attempt to reconcile others to God and encourage them to grow in Christian maturity. As such, this text should prove beneficial to all Christians acting as ambassadors for Christ Jesus in all one-anothering relationships. My hope is that this exploration into the development of a distinctly Christian psychology will enable the readers to have a keener understanding of God's will for their lives and enable them to be more effective as they one-another for the kingdom of God. The goal of this text is to provide a general overview of a cohesive

Christian psychology. Many Christians have come to believe that all the nuggets of wisdom in the Bible have already been discovered. I hope the reader is encouraged to search for new answers by asking new questions. As we explore these areas of interest we can be encouraged by the words found in 2 Timothy 3:16,17, "All Scripture is God breathed and is useful for teaching, rebuking, correcting and training in righteousness, so that the man of God may be thoroughly equipped for every good work."

CHAPTER 1

A DISTINCT CHRISTIAN PSYCHOLOGY

Christianity and Psychology

The word psychology comes from the Greek words *psyche* (soul) and *logos* (word) and literally means "soul-talk" or the study of the human soul. While both Christians and psychologists are much interested in developing a better understanding of the human soul, the relationship between Christianity and psychology has often been less than harmonious. The conflict experienced between Christians and the discipline of psychology is primarily the result of opposing worldviews. Many respected Christian psychologists, philosophers, and theologians have written books delineating their thoughts concerning the appropriate relationship that Christians should have with the field of psychology. Some have set forth models of integration, and others have argued that the Bible and psychology are enemies, and, therefore, it is not possible to integrate the two. Even with this history of animosity, many Christians have concluded that modern psychology has developed ideas that could prove beneficial to Christians as they attempt to deal with human problems addressed by various psychological theories. Finding a reasonable place to stand on the issue is a challenge for any Christian who has a serious interest in the study of the human soul. Accurate discernment of psychological information is of primary importance.

As a starting point, we must recognize that there are two qualitatively distinct branches of study within the discipline of psychology that intersect with a Christian psychology. The first branch of study, often referred to as general psychology, contains a treasure trove of scientific data developed through sound empirical methodology. Research in general psychology proposes and tests a narrowly defined hypothesis, examining a very simple relationship (predictive or causal) between two variables without much concern for the bigger picture. General psychology generates very small pieces of data regarding neural functioning, sensation, perception, cognitive processes, problem solving, motivation, emotion, learning, memory, and much more, with limited attention given to the way in which each of these pieces of data relate to one another or to the phenomenological functioning of human beings as whole persons. These small pieces of data often accumulate into a large body of empirical knowledge, called a scientific theory, regarding some aspect of human functioning. For example, there have been literally thousands of studies conducted on the functioning of the human memory system. These cumulative studies allow us to develop a theoretical system of memory that is both valid and reliable. The same holds true for empirical studies examining the processes by which our sense organs perceive the world around us, as well as, the transmission of that sensory information via the nervous system. One might say that general psychology attempts to discover, through empirical methodologies, the distinctive mechanisms that support the soul.

The specific worldview of the researcher, the most problematic component for the Christian, is irrelevant to the research process and findings. While the researcher may speak from a specific worldview as they interpret their findings in the discussion section of the research results, that same worldview would confound the results if it were to influence the actual research in any way. Nevertheless, this interpretation often contradicts Scripture and thereby creates problems for Christians. It is important to separate the scientific research from the accompanying interpretation of the researcher.

Let me provide an example to clarify the potential for disparity between empirical research and the interpretation of that research. Silverman and Weinberger (1985) summarized a body of empirical research that focused on the "powerful wishes, typically unconscious, in many adults, for a state of oneness with another person" (p. 188). The authors concluded that numerous studies had demonstrated that "activating the theme of oneness produced ameliorative effects for (relatively differentiated) schizophrenics that were not produced when other, even very similar, themes were activated" (p. 192). Consequent studies had demonstrated that this same theme of oneness also lowered anxiety levels for normal people. So, to this point we have empirical research that demonstrates a cause and effect relationship. A "theme of oneness" (cause) was introduced to the subjects and the effect was lessening the characteristic symptoms in schizophrenics and lowering anxiety levels in normal people. When the authors interpreted what this relationship signified, they did so from a perspective consistent with their worldview.

They concluded that the research supported the universal desire that one has for a symbiotic relationship with one's mother, which has been characterized to the extreme of an unconscious longing to be back in the mother's womb. The only logical connection between the empirically demonstrated cause and effect relationship and their subjective conclusion is the agreement that conclusion has with their specific worldview. A Christian worldview interpretation makes as much sense and is just as valid. As Christians, we hold that man has been alienated from, and longs to be reconciled to, his Creator. The means by which this reconciliation is accomplished is through Jesus Christ. More specifically, to be reconciled to God we must become part of the "body of Christ" (1 Corinthians 12:27). This alienation creates a void in every human soul that exists apart from God and the subsequent drive toward "oneness" is directed toward oneness with Jesus Christ, or possibly the unity of all believers, not one's mother. As you can see, the scientifically demonstrated relationship is congruent with Scripture and could possibly provide insights as we explore this doctrine of unity. The secular interpretation of psychological research is often troublesome for Christians and can generally be disregarded without confounding the research. I believe it was this perspective that kept me grounded in my graduate studies. I had a steadfast attitude that I was there to learn the science of psychology from the premier academics in the field. I was not there to be mentored on how to live my personal life or to blindly adopt their worldview interpretations of the science.

While general psychology is by far the broadest field of study within the discipline of psychology, it is "clinical psychology" that generates the most attention and is most problematic for Christians. Unfortunately, it is this second area that addresses issues most relevant to a Christian psychology. Clinical psychology consists of a collection of theoretical systems that attempt to explain the functioning of whole persons and the appropriate manner in which a therapist should interact and progress in a relationship with a client based on the presuppositions of a specific theoretical system (i.e., psychoanalytic, person-centered etc.). These theoretical systems should more accurately be referred to as hypothetical systems because they are not based on a cumulative body of empirical research. Instead, they are created from multiple worldviews and their respective presuppositions, and structured from sources ranging from subjective personal experience to simple observation. Not only do these theories of psychotherapy lack substantial empirical support from the body of research in general psychology, the body of research in general psychology often contradicts the specific assumptions made by those theories.

In his *Manifesto for a Science of Clinical Psychology*, McFall (1991) stated that he believed "we must make a greater effort to differentiate between scientific and pseudoscientific clinical psychology and to hasten the day when the former replaces the later" (p. 76). In an attempt to improve the credibility of psychotherapeutic systems, Division 12 (clinical psychology) of the American Psychological Association (APA) has collected information regarding what it refers to as empirically supported treatments (EST's). The result is a concise collection of limited empirical evidence supporting both cognitive and behavioral treatments for a small number of narrowly defined problems. The APA web site's frequently asked questions section acknowledges that many well-known forms of psychotherapy (i.e., psychodynamic, existential, person-centered, reality, etc.) are not listed as EST's. It attempts to clarify this discrepancy by stating that this omission only indicates a lack of empirical support and does not signify that these theories are ineffective. The APA acknowledges that the need for empirical support for practiced theories of psychotherapy is not only desired, it is a necessity. This concern is specifically addressed in a report (Chambless, 1993) adopted by the Division 12 Board of the APA which states, " In light of the large number of APA members who practice psychodynamic psychotherapy, in the interest of the profession and the public, we conclude that it is crucial that more efficacy evidence on the outcome of psychodynamic therapies for specific disorders be obtained if this clinically verified treatment is to survive in today's market" (p. 2). A decade later, in an update (Woody et al., 2005) on EST's, it was found that "many widely used treatments have yet to be rigorously tested" (p. 5) and that most professional programs in counseling and psychology do not include training in the current list of EST's. The conclusion drawn is that graduate programs in counseling and clinical psychology have a long way to go before they will accurately represent the scientific basis of the discipline of psychology (p. 11). It's fairly obvious that the division of psychology that seeks to understand and facilitate change in the human soul is not functioning at a scientific level. The logical conclusion is that these theories, or hypotheses, lack scientific reliability and validity.

Let me make a few summary statements of my personal view regarding the relationship between psychology and Christianity. First, the objective data produced through scientific psychological research is typically consistent with Biblical teaching. God created humans and humans are the subjects that psychology attempts to understand. Inasmuch as Scripture specifies the nature of the relationships of interest, it will be consistent with the empirical data gleaned from psychological research. Second, there are two forms of error that are always present in experimental scientific research. Systematic error is a result of the imperfect methodologies used and affects the accuracy of the research. Random error is a result of the uniqueness of the subjects being studied and affects the precision of research results. To integrate the infallible Word of God and the science of psychology, with its inherent error, is like mixing oil and vinegar; you mix them together and it won't be long till they separate again. As such, it is reasonable to conclude that psychological research should not be used to support Scripture, though Scripture can support psychological research. It is better to view psychological research as data that has the potential to augment our understanding of Scripture. Third, due to varying worldviews, both the subjective interpretation of data in general psychology and the theories of psychotherapy as a whole, may or may not be consistent with Biblical teaching. In other words, psychology is not an enemy of Christianity, but some psychologists are. Finally, God's Word is not only sufficient; it is necessary in defining the human soul and providing direction for the redefinition of the human soul. Put another way, once sin entered into the world and infected the soul of man, God did not leave us in a state of limbo for thousands of years waiting for the birth of Wilhelm Wundt or Sigmund Freud, the fathers of psychology and psychiatry respectively, to save us.

Only the Word of God can inform us to the appropriate definition of the soul and provide direction for the appropriate redefinition of the soul. Every man has a soul, and general psychology provides insights that can guide us as we strive to live effectively. However, if we truly want to develop the spiritual and earthly components of our souls and become what God originally intended us to be, we must seek direction from the Creator Himself. Jesus came, not to take the life one has and not to remediate the life one has but to give abundantly more life, spiritual life, life that overflows (see John 10:10). Only God's Word can accurately define what one is and provide what is necessary to redefine one to become what God created her or him to be.

A Distinct Christian Psychology

Based on the current and historical relationship between psychology (specifically theories of psychotherapy) and Christianity, the ideal solution for Christianity would be to develop a distinct Christian psychology. Many Christian psychologists and counselors with whom I have talked over the past twenty years considered this idea preposterous. However, in recent years there has been an increase in the number of respected voices and an increase in the unity of those voices for the development of a distinct Christian psychology. A growing number of Christian psychologists, philosophers and theologians are aggressively attempting to meet the challenge of a Christian psychology and inspire others with a similar interest to join with them in this venture. As part of this effort a new organization, the Society for Christian Psychology, was formed to provide a place for dialog and discussion in pursuit of its mission statement: "The Society exists to promote the development of a distinctly Christian psychology (including theory, research, and practice) that is based on a Christian vision of human nature" (Johnson, 2004b, p. 1). The ideas generated by this society have been beneficial for clarifying three foundational issues relevant to the formation of a Christian psychology. First, what is the rationale that will support a Christian psychology? Second, what sources would be acceptable in the development of a Christian psychology? And, finally, what might a Christian psychology look like?

For Christians, the general rationale for a Christian psychology would involve a narrative such as the following. In the beginning, Adam and Eve walked in the

Garden of Eden in full fellowship with God, their Creator. They functioned physically, mentally, and spiritually according to God's design and as such were in complete harmony with the will of God. Then one dreadful day, through conscious choice and a free will, man disobeyed God and, thereby, committed sin against God. The evil associated with this sin corrupted the whole man so that he was no longer functioning in harmony with his Creator. In essence, the glasses through which Adam and Eve had once been fortunate to view God and His creation had shattered. Now, everything they sensed and perceived was distorted in some way. To reconcile man to Himself, God sent His only Son Jesus Christ, to become a sacrifice for sin. Through the blood of Jesus Christ, man could once again be reconciled to God. Through the instruction of the Word of God and the power of the Holy Spirit, man could bring the distorted glasses that had warped his view of God and the world for so long, back to optical purity. Man once again could be what God intended him to be, but only through the power of the Living Word. For most Christians, this truth is self-evident and provides enough rationale for the development of a Christian psychology; however, it might be beneficial to look at the rationale for a Christian psychology from a perspective that is more formal.

In *Locating Christian Psychology,* Johnson (2004a) finds that Christian philosopher Alvin Plantinga "has written a well-structured argument for the rationality of holding to specifically Christian beliefs (in creating a Christian psychology) even though other rational persons disagree."

> He (Plantinga) has argued (1993, p. 3ff) that it is rational to assume the following: 1) the human mind is a belief producing mechanism; 2) the human mind produces beliefs according to its design plan; 3) if it is producing

> beliefs according to its design plan, it is properly functioning; 4) if it is properly functioning, it will yield reliable knowledge; and 5) if it is not functioning properly, it may not yield reliable knowledge.
>
> In his more recent book (2000, p. 201), Plantinga has argued that, according to Christianity, 1) the design plan of the human mind has been vitiated by sin which has caused damage to its knowing capacities and so compromised its ability to know certain things (e.g., knowledge of self and God), and 2) one of the gifts of the Holy Spirit is the restoration of those knowing capacities lost by sin. (pp. 12- 14)

Johnson (2004b) states, "If Plantinga is right, the Christian psychologist is also within his or her epistemic rights to hold to specifically Christian beliefs and allow them to influence his or her research, theory-building, and counseling practice, regardless of the 'discourse rules' and 'ethical standards' of the modernist majority who dominate the field of psychology currently. Therefore, the one issue that many would consider a weakness of Christian psychology–that it is founded on the presuppositions of Scripture–is in reality its strength" (pp. 13,14). Scripture provides a cohesive rationale for Christian psychology, and a cohesive rationale is lacking in the theories of psychotherapy because the presuppositions of those theories have no foundation. It is much like the university professor that informs the class that the planetary system took shape when the gravitational properties of dust particles floating through space caused them to accumulate into larger particles. These particles collided with other large particles and at some point what we now know as the planetary systems were formed. How many students in universities accept that hypothesis without ever questioning the origins of the dust particles or even the origin of space itself?

In addition to providing a rationale for a Christian psychology, Plantinga's argument also broadens the field of possible sources from which a Christian psychology can be constructed. At first thought, one might conclude that Scripture is the only valid source for a Christian psychology; however, based on Plantinga's argument and arguments set forth by theologians concerning man's ability to know truth, the possible sources for a Christian psychology would include both Scripture, which Christians should rightfully place full confidence in as the inspired Word of God, as well as, writings by Christian psychologists, philosophers, and theologians that explore psychological themes within Scripture. Because Christians have the indwelling of the Holy Spirit and because one of the gifts of the Holy Spirit is to restore man's ability to know truth that was lost by sin (see 1 Corinthians 2:10-13), it is reasonable to assume that Christians can generate ideas consistent with Scripture. It is this very premise that supports the writing of devotionals, commentaries, and even sermons. While these two sources would be self-evident to most Christians, I believe there is a third source, with a corresponding rationale, that should also be considered of value as we pursue the development of a Christian psychology. This source would include the research and writings of non-Christians searching for answers to questions with a psychological and spiritual theme. The rationale for this addition is that God reveals Himself through His creation (see Romans 1:20) and this general revelation is visible to all mankind. Non-Christians (created in the image of God) exploring the inner workings of the human soul (created in the image of God) will discover patterns complimentary with the original design plan of the Creator. It is important to understand the relative value and proper application of each of these sources in the development of a Christian psychology. While each of these sources can provide insight, you will discover that I will generate most of my observations in this text directly from Scripture.

The final question then is; what would a Christian psychology look like? This question is difficult to answer since we are in the process of working toward a Christian psychology. Roberts (1997) identifies five key elements that are typical of what a Christian psychology might include.

> A psychology is a systematically integrated body of thought and practice that includes the following five elements:
>
> **1.** An account of basic human nature answers two kinds of questions. First, what is the teleology of human nature? Second, how are human persons structured, most basically?
> **2.** A psychology will sketch, or at a minimum imply, a set of personality traits that characterize a fully functioning, mature person.
> **3.** A psychology will describe the successful development of personality.
> **4.** The obverse of elements two and three is a psychology's diagnostic scheme.
> **5.** A psychology need not actually include a psychotherapy–a set of interventions that aim to correct or prevent unhealthy patterns of interaction and traits of personality–but the development of one is natural, and psychologies that arise out of the practices of life can be expected to have at least a rudimentary therapy. (pp. 76, 77)

In addition, Roberts (2003) believes that the main work of a Christian psychology at this stage "is constructive–that is, just trying to figure out what the Christian tradition says about psychological questions. This is a primarily hermeneutical or interpretive task, a matter of reading the tradition carefully and trying to clarify and perhaps systematize what it says. For this part of the task, scientific research is less important than historical and biblical research" (p. 9).

The need is evident, the rationale and guidelines have been structured, and we are off on a new venture, the construction of a distinctly Christian psychology. While it appears to be an overwhelming task, a statement attributed to Einstein concerning the possibility of understanding the universe encourages me: "The thing that is incomprehensible is that it will be comprehensible." What I propose in this text is that the parameters of the human soul are knowable and comprehensible and that understanding these parameters will allow us to define the current state of an individual soul and guide us in the proper direction for a redefining of that soul. By defining the parameters of the soul, one essentially defines the parameters of a Christian psychology.

CHAPTER 2

THE BASIC STRUCTURE OF MAN

The first question we will address is, "How is man structured, most basically?" Scripture tells us that man is a living soul. Scripture also tells us that man possesses a heart, spirit and mind. Theology texts and Bible dictionaries sufficiently define the constructs of the human heart, spirit, soul and mind. A Christian psychology, however, will be more interested in the relationship that exists between these theological constructs. We will revisit these theological constructs, paying particular attention to characteristics that might inform regarding ordinal relationship, to generate a new perspective of how man functions as a whole. Hopefully, this will generate new insights that will provide guidance as we strive, in a practical way, to live closer to the will of God. As we focus on the relationships between the human heart, spirit, soul and mind we will create a kind of taxonomy. Taxonomy is an organizational system that classifies items of interest by type and ordinal relationship. Thus, our goal is to examine the characteristics of each construct to identify its type and then place each construct in an ordered relationship. It should be noted that I have no intention to separate these constructs, only to distinguish and relate.

The specific question we are asking is this. How are the theological constructs of the human heart, spirit, soul and mind implicated by type and ordinal relationship when a person is functioning at the highest level of consciousness that separates man from animals? In other words, how are these constructs implicated when a human being is engaged in reasoned, purposeful behavior? For each of these terms we will distinguish the constructs by examining their characteristics. We will note if Scripture uses the term in reference to God, man or animal and as a material or immaterial entity. For the later, we accept that Scripture clearly supports some form of substance dualism (i.e., man is both material and immaterial, corporeal and incorporeal). My original hypothesis was that reasoned, purposeful behavior flows from the heart to the spirit to the soul; however, when I attempted to validate this ordinal relationship with Scripture I discovered there is a slightly different progression.

I would like to refer the reader to an analogy for clarification as we progress in our understanding of the relationship between the human heart, spirit, soul and mind. I will borrow an analogy from Plato's chariot allegory from his dialog Phaedrus (sections 246a-254e), for this purpose. Plato likened the soul to a chariot being pulled by a black horse and a white horse. According to Plato, the two horses represent the competing tendencies of the soul. The white horse is long-necked, turns easily, is well behaved and runs without a whip. The white horse represents the aesthetic and selfless tendencies of the soul. The black horse is short-necked, difficult to control, badly bred and troublesome. The black horse represents the soul's passions, appetites and sensual nature. For Plato, the charioteer represents intellect, reason, or the part of the soul that must guide the soul to truth. We will revisit and modify this analogy as we progress in developing our taxonomy.

The Soul

Scripture uses the term soul (Hebrew, *nephesh*; Greek, *psyche*) in reference to man and animal and infrequently to God. For those who have not studied the Scriptural usage of these terms the fact that the term soul is used in reference to animals often comes as a surprise, however, *nephesh* is used four times in Genesis 1 in reference to animals (see Genesis 1:20, 21, 24 & 30) before the creation of man is recorded in Genesis 2. When *nephesh* or *psyche* is used in Scripture in reference to animals it is often translated with the words life or need. For example, depending on the translation, Proverbs 12:10 states, "A righteous man cares for the needs/life/soul (*nephesh*) of his animal." The term soul refers to the general life of a living creature or what we often refer to as personhood in humans. The soul is defined by acquired knowledge in that it is shaped by all the biographical information that constitutes one's personal narrative. Everything you know, both implicitly and explicitly, is stored in the soul. It is this personally distinctive collection of information, or experiences, that makes each individual unique. The human soul is the storehouse of one's memories and experiences and represents one's current state of being and future potential. According to Brown (1986), the concept of soul "embraces the whole natural being and life of man for which he concerns himself and which he takes constant care" (v. 3, p. 683). Given these characteristics, what would constitute the soul of God? Well, God is omniscient and His soul would contain all that is good. Consequently, anything righteous will be congruent with the soul of God and cause His soul to delight and rejoice (Isaiah 42:1; Matthew 12:18) while anything evil will be dissonant with the soul of God and be loathed and abhorred by His soul (Leviticus 26:30; Zechariah 11:8). Unlike God's soul, man's soul contains both good and evil. For this reason man often experiences opposing tendencies of the soul. The soul develops in relationship toward or away from God. It is the soul that sins (see Ezekiel 18:4), the soul that is saved (see Job 33:28), and the soul that matures spiritually.

An animal soul is material in that it is fully a product of biological processes. A human soul also relies on biological processes and will be material inasmuch as the human soul has in common with an animal soul. Indeed, one of the central questions asked by theologians concerning the human soul is, "How can a material soul survive death?" So then, where do we place the soul, in ordinal relationship, when a person is engaged in reasoned purposeful behavior? An animal soul acts on instinct and impulse. A human soul can act in a similar, impulsive manner. When engaged in reasoned, purposeful behavior something must precede a simple stimulus-response type of impulse. Therefore, we will place the soul at ordinal position three. Referring back to our chariot analogy, the two horses represent the often-competing tendencies (impulses) of the soul. We will be examining the two tendencies of the soul in more detail at a later point.

The Heart

We now turn our attention to the human heart (Hebrew, *leb*; Greek, *kardia*). Scripture uses the term heart; in it's spiritual sense, only in reference to God and man. The nature of the heart is spiritual and it possesses the foundational qualities of goodness, virtue and moral excellence. The heart is intimately related to man's spirit. Heart refers to the seat of man's thoughts, passions, desires, appetites, affections, endeavors, intelligence and understanding. According to Brown (1986) heart denotes "the seat of intellectual and spiritual life. The powers of the spirit, reason, and will have their seat in the heart" (v. 2, p. 182). Scripture tells us that sin is first committed in the heart (Matthew 5:28), forgiveness must come from the heart (Matthew 18:35) and the word of God is sown and must come to fruition in the heart (Luke 8:11-15). Robinson (1926) notes that Paul uses heart in fifteen cases to refer to the inner life in general, in thirteen cases to refer to the seat of emotional states of consciousness, in eleven cases to refer to the seat of intellectual activities and in thirteen cases to refer to the seat of volition (p. 106). At this point it appears obvious the concept of heart will occupy the first ordinal position in the taxonomy and that reasoned purposeful behavior begins in the heart. Placing the heart within our chariot analogy will take a little extra thought. The heart is not the charioteer that controls the horses, but instead, is what provides direction for the charioteer. The charioteer's heart would be equivalent to his predisposition or where his allegiance lies. Is the charioteer Athenian or Persian? To whom does the charioteer's loyalty belong? This will dictate where he guides the horses and whom he fights with and against in battle.

The Spirit

We now turn our attention to one of the most interesting constructs, the human spirit (Hebrew, *ruwach;* Greek, *pneuma*). Scripture uses the term spirit in reference to both God and man. Scripture does not use the term spirit in reference to animals. The spirit is that which man has in common with God. Cottrell (2002) states, "Whatever the image of God turns out to be, it must be something that is both in God and not in animals" (p. 50). While man's spirit is a gift from God and one thing which man has in common with God, the spirit in man is not divine. The spirit in man can prompt both righteousness and evil (see Hosea 4:12; Isaiah 29:24). As the name implies, the nature of the spirit is spiritual. Scripture tells us that man's spirit is a gift from God and the eternal part of man (see Zechariah 12:1). When Scripture speaks of beings that have died and passed from this world, they are referred to as spirits in all but one instance. In Revelation 6:9 John writes that he "saw under the altar the souls of those who had been slain because of the Word of God and the testimony they had maintained." In this instance, John refers to those he saw as souls rather than spirits because he referred to their martyrdom, an earthly life experience and part of their personhood.

Scripture tells us that man's spirit is "the lamp of the Lord searching all the innermost parts of his being" (Psalms 20:27) and that it is "the spirit of man that knows the thoughts of man" (1 Corinthians 2:11). In Scripture, the concept of spirit is intimately related to the concept of heart. Brown (1986) states that, "Spirit often stands alongside heart. The difference is that the heart dwells within man, having indeed been created by God, but it is not a fleeting, oscillating gift like the breath of man's spirit. Heart refers to a man's aims and resolves. Spirit refers to the direction in which a man's vitality flows, the self-expression involved in his behavior" (v. 3, p. 691). When engaged in reasoned, purposeful behavior man's heart > spirit equals man's desire > activity. Theoretically, the core beliefs of cognitive psychology are located in the heart and the spirit prompts resulting actions. In virtue psychology the cardinal virtues are of the heart and the spirit prompts expression through personality. It is the spirit in man that assesses and acts on information in the soul. Man's spirit is the source of man's agency, where agency refers to the capacity of human beings to make self-directed choices and engage in reasoned purposeful behavior. Agency is often contrasted to natural forces, which include instincts, impulses and automaticity, which are causes involving non-cognitive, deterministic behavior. In the taxonomy, the spirit occupies ordinal position number two. The spirit flows in the direction set by the heart (ordinal position one) and acts on the information stored in the soul (ordinal position three).

The human spirit is a simple, immaterial essence and possesses the power of knowing, desiring, deciding and acting. Brown (1986) notes that the Greek word *pneuma* (spirit) is made up of two parts. "*Pneu* (root) - denotes the dynamic movement of air. *Ma* (suffix) - denotes the result of this action, namely, air set in motion considered as a special substance and with an underlying stress on its inherent power" (v. 3, p. 689). Building on Brown's etymology, the human spirit is like the wind in the sails of a ship. The wind represents the spirit while the sails represent the soul. Just as it is the inherent power of "air set in motion" that moves the ship on the surface of the water, it is the human spirit that activates the human soul when a person is engaged in reasoned, purposeful behavior. In our chariot analogy, the charioteer represents the spirit. When the charioteer is passive or incapacitated the black horse runs unfettered and there is a negative outcome. In the New Testament evil spirits assume power over an individual's personal agency. When the evil spirit is cast out, the individual's spirit regains control of personal agency. Conversely, when the charioteer reins in the black horse and allows the white horse to run unfettered there is a good outcome. Likewise, when a human spirit is activating the part of the soul that is congruent with things of God (truth), there is a righteous outcome. This may very well be the central message of John

4:23 that we are to worship "the Father in spirit and truth," and Romans 1:9 that we are to serve "God in spirit and the gospel of His Son." It is worthwhile to note, that while we can distinguish between the spirit and soul they actually form an integrated whole (see Hebrews 4:12), or what Scripture refers to as the human mind.

The Mind

The mind (Hebrew, *leb*; Greek, *nous* or *dianoia*) is used in reference to God, man and animals. The nature of the mind is both spiritual and material in man and material in animals. For man, the characteristics of the mind include judgment, discernment, thoughtful reason and purposeful behavior. Scripture tells us that man's spirit is part of the mind (see Ephesians 4:23) so the human mind is the totality of the spirit and soul functioning at their fullest potential (engaged in reasoned purposeful behavior). Brown (1986) states, the "mind expresses not merely an activity of the intellect, but also a movement of the will. The concept of mind comes nearest to the concept of wisdom" (v. 2, p. 620). The animal mind, not possessing a spirit, functions through soul activity alone. When an animal soul acts we call the resulting behavior instinctive or impulsive. The human soul, acting without prompting from the spirit, can also act impulsively. This impulsive behavior is sometimes referred to as soulish behavior. Recall that King Nebuchadnezzar (see Daniel 4:16) was given the mind of an animal and lived by instinct and impulse. When God restored King Nebuchadnezzar, and he regained his own mind, he was once again able to reason. Reason is a function of spirit-soul interaction. Many theologians state that it is because of man's possession of *nous* (mind) that humans are made in the image of God. Indeed, when we critically examine the characteristics theologians list as indicative of being created in the image of God (personal consciousness, intellectual capacity, volitional capacity, moral and ethical capacity, creativity, etc.), we discover that each relies on the spirit-soul interaction that characterizes the higher levels of consciousness. As Paul states, "Those that are after the flesh [predisposition of the heart] mind [spirit-soul interaction] the things of the flesh and those that are after the Spirit [predisposition of the heart] mind [spirit-soul interaction] the things of the Spirit" (Romans 8:5).

The Spirit-Soul Relation

Now we consider a most important relationship as we revisit the spirit-soul relation that is instrumental in forming relationships with the external world. Man's spirit is spirit, man's soul is soul, and the synthesis of the two is the uniquely human self. Kierkegaard (1941) states, "the self is a relation that relates itself to itself" (p. 13). Benner & Hill (1999) note the fact that man can have a relationship with himself is unique among earthly creatures (p. 1077). It is through this self-relation, a relation unique to humans, that the self is capable of relating to other people and to God. The ability to choose between spiritual and earthly relationships, the often-competing tendencies of the soul, lies in our capacity for a self-relationship. Think of it this way. An embryo exists in the womb as a synthesis of spirit and soul, and it will exist as spirit and soul into eternity even though the soul (formed by earthly life experiences) has not developed. Humans have a very real, eternal existence (spirit) apart from personhood (soul). You might think of the spirit as the beginning reference point of your personhood. We will call this reference point the "I" which represents the individual at his or her most basic, spiritual (in the eternal sense) level. This "I" is like a mental "eye," or the illuminator of the soul, that engages the developing soul through self-examination and the world through the context of the soul. As one's soul matures, the spirit or the "I" illuminates and ponders the developing soul, a collection of spiritual and earthly relationships. The evidence for this concept is biblically sound and logically supported. As Paul writes, "For who among men knows the thoughts of a man except the spirit of the man which is in him" (1 Corinthians 2:11)? In addition, the Psalmist writes, "The spirit of man is the lamp of the Lord, searching all the innermost parts of his being" (Psalms 20:27). These two components, spirit and soul, function together as a synthesis. The integrated relation of the spirit and soul constitutes the totality of one's personhood–the self. (See figure 2-1.) This synthesis is more complete, more abundant, for those who develop their soul through relationship with God and things grounded in God than for those who simply define themselves through relationship to the world and things grounded in the world.

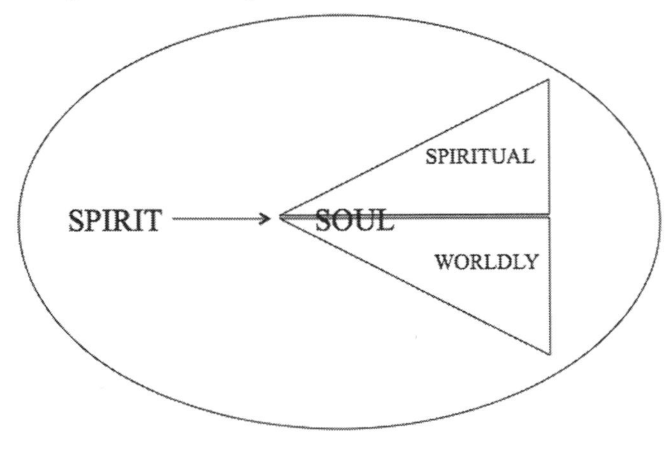

Figure 2-1

The Bible speaks of the necessity of the self to relate itself to itself through the process of self-examination (see 1 Corinthians 11:28; 2 Corinthians 13:5). Additionally, the fact that a person can be content or discontent with his or her personhood proves this concept of self-relation. Are you totally satisfied with who you are? Most of us feel that there is always need for personal improvement. The fact that a state of contentedness or discontentedness is possible within an individual demonstrates that there is a relation between two. Two perspectives, a self, relating itself to itself, are necessary to experience disparity. There can be agreement or disagreement, consonance or dissonance, between the spirit and the soul. A comparison may be worth considering. Scripture tells us that animals have souls (see Genesis 1:24; 2:7), but Scripture does not attribute a spirit to animals. Animals have a collection of life experiences and learn through association (relationships) similar to humans. However, researchers believe that some animals may have a limited capacity for self-awareness in that they are conscious of their existence, but they do not have the capacity to relate to themselves as humans do. A self-relationship or spirit-soul relation is a quality unique to humans. A pet does not lie around wondering if it is reaching its full potential or pondering whom it really is. Animals lack the reference point or the "I" necessary for self-examination. Animals also lack the spirit that man possesses.

In *Mere Christianity,* C. S. Lewis (1952) provides an example that clearly demonstrates this spirit-soul relation. Lewis writes of a human tendency toward opposing soul relationships, spiritual and worldly, and the spirit (what Lewis calls the Moral Law) that must decide between the two. I have inserted the contrasting soul relationships of [spiritual and worldly] and [spirit] where applicable.

> Suppose you hear a cry for help from a man in danger. You will probably feel two desires - one desire to give help (due to your herd instinct)[spiritual], the other a desire to keep out of danger (due to the instinct for self-preservation) [worldly]. But you will find inside of you, in addition to these two impulses, a third thing [spirit] which tells you that you ought to follow the impulse to help, and suppress the impulse to run away. Now this thing [spirit] that judges between two instincts, that decides which should be encouraged, cannot itself be either of them.
>
> If two instincts are in conflict, and there is nothing in the creature's mind except those two instincts, obviously the stronger of the two must win. But at those moments when we are most conscious of the Moral Law, it [spirit] usually tells us to side with the weaker of the two impulses. You probably want to be safe much more than you want to help the man who is drowning: but the Moral Law [spirit] tells you to help him all the same. And surely it often tells us to try to make the right impulse stronger than it naturally is. (pp. 9-10)

The spirit may well be the seat of one's conscience. Paul writes that even those who have no access to God's Word still have His Law written in their hearts to guide them (see Romans 2:14, 15). Even so, not everyone in the situation described by Lewis will choose to do what is right. Others may not even consider the choices and simply act in a way that ensures their safety. It is possible for a person to act without guidance from the spirit-soul relation. These actions are impulsive (Lewis used the term instinctive) and require no thought or reason (see 2 Peter 2:12, Jude 1:10). Uzzah impulsively put out his hand and took hold of the Ark of the Covenant to keep it from falling. God's "anger burned against Uzzah" due to his disobedience, and God struck him dead (see 2 Samuel 6:6). Peter, possibly from an impulse to protect Jesus and himself, drew his sword, and lopped off the ear of the high priest's servant. Consequently, Peter was rebuked by Jesus (see John 18:10).

When I worked at the psychiatric hospital, many of the patients had problems controlling impulsive behavior. It is known that many disorders including mood disorders, eating disorders and substance abuse disorders are characterized by a lack of impulse control. These patients found it difficult to exercise self-control over their impulses and would respond immediately, impulsively, to both internal and external stimuli without first thinking through the situation and following that assessment with informed behaviors. Acting by impulse cannot please God, because God requires that we act by faith, and faith requires reasoning (see 2 Corinthians 5:7, Romans 14:23). How many times have you acted by impulse and immediately been aware that you had acted in a way not consistent with your real, heart-felt desires? We are to "take captive every thought and make it obedient to Christ" (2 Corinthians 10:5). God works in us not just to act according to His good purpose but to "will and to act according to his good purpose" (Philippians 2:13). The soul is the storehouse of knowledge. When the spirit and soul interact, reasoning or rational thinking is the outcome. This is accomplished as the spirit applies specific principles to the information available in the soul that are relevant to the current issue thereby making a reasonable and informed decision. The specific principles the spirit uses to analyze the relevant information may be spiritual or worldly. Faced with an identical situation, one person may reason within the context of "loving one's neighbor" and another person may reason in the context of "looking out for number one." In other words, not all reasoning leads to righteous behavior.

While it is common for problems presented by a client in counseling to be the product of impulsive behavior, it is just as common to see problems manifest themselves due to improper motives of the heart and faulty reasoning. Sometimes the rules applied are worldly or based on common sense, which may or may not be compatible with Scriptural precedents. Cognitive therapy is a secular therapy that relies on the human ability to think rationally. The Achilles heal of cognitive therapy is that not all people agree on what is rational. Consequently, because cognitive therapy is based on rational thought, therapy will only be as good as the therapist is rational. Applying biblical principles to the reasoning process provides a standard that is acceptable to Christians. Wisdom indicates reasoning, and we know that there is wisdom from above and wisdom from below (see James 3:15-17). Sadly, evil people often use the spirit-soul relationship to "invent ways of doing evil" (Romans 1:30).

Referring back to Lewis' example, there appears to be three ways in which one can interact with the external world. The third entity of which Lewis speaks of (the spirit) may never get involved, and the person could impulsively seek safety. Or, it is possible that the third entity (the spirit) may relate to the soul, ponder the right thing to do, and then rationalize through this self-relation that someone else will come along who is a better swimmer and more capable of helping, logically concluding that it is best to seek safety. Finally, a spirit sensitive to the Moral Law (i.e., love your neighbor) could encourage a person to act in a way that is morally right, and provide a corresponding rationale, even though the impulse to do so is the weaker of the two.

Much of the tension between the spiritual and worldly tendencies of the soul can be attributed to the fact that the soul develops (builds relationships) caring for the both the mental self (psychological and spiritual needs) and the physical self (biological needs). Scripture asserts (see Mark 12:31) that one's soul is attentive to one's mental and physical needs and naturally acts to meet those needs (i.e., the Christian love of oneself). The constant, natural attention given to meeting the needs of the physical self defines much of one's soul. Tensions surface when a person discovers that there are inappropriate ways to meet psychological and physical needs, through sinful acts and excesses, and consequently desires these alternatives to God's will even though the alternatives cannot fully satisfy. The human spirit may know and be willing to act in a way that is consistent with the will of God but the flesh (worldly, material soul and body) may have developed stalwart, habitual relationships that counteract that will (see Matthew 26:38).

Before we advance, I want to call the reader's attention to an additional insight by Lewis (1952) that emphasizes the importance of spirit-driven, reasoned behavior. Once again I have inserted clarifications relevant to the topic at hand where applicable.

> Human beings judge one another by their external actions. God judges them by their internal choices [made by the spirit]. That is why Christians are told not to judge. We see only the results, which a man's choices make out of his raw material [state of his material soul]. But God does not judge him on the raw material at all, but on what he has done with it. Most of man's psychological makeup is probably due to his body [material]: when his body dies all that will fall off him, and the real central man [his spirit], the thing that chose [his spirit], that made the best or worst out of his material [soul], will stand naked. All sorts of nice things which we thought our own, but were really

> due to good digestion, will fall off some of us [material soul]: all sorts of nasty things which were due to complexes or bad health will fall off others [material soul]. We shall then, for the first time, see every one as he really was [a spirit that could choose]. There will be surprises. (pp. 86-87)

The fact that we have the capacity to be self-relational facilitates an awareness of self over a time continuum. We can understand who we have been, who we are now, and can appreciate who we can become potentially. In essence then, we can define the soul (past and present) and think about the process of redefining the soul (future). A core premise in psychology is that the best predictor of future behavior is past behavior. This statement often raises objections from Christians because it causes some to jump to the conclusion that the premise is deterministic. In reality, the claim is not that the past is a perfect predictor of the future, but that it is only the best predictor available. When I discuss this principle in a class, I rephrase the statement to convey a more optimistic, and—I affirm—a more Biblical, perspective. I rephrase the principle to "Your present is your future because it just became your past." So, the best predictor of future behavior is indeed past behavior. More specifically, the best predictor of future behavior is the most recent past; that past that was just the present. Your past was actually your present a moment ago. By building new relationships now, in the present, you effectively change your past and, therefore, predict a new future. James wrote that you should "consider it pure joy . . . whenever you face trials" because testing, in the present, provides an opportunity for you to engage in reasoned, purposeful behavior and to mature through perseverance (see James 1:2-5). Perseverance is simply continuing through trials, in the present, until you successfully change relationships. These relationships will be formed by faith with a reliance on God and His directives for your life. That is the essence of my classroom statement.

The spirit knows the thoughts of man and is the lamp of the Lord. The soul is the storehouse of earthly experiences. Based on those two biblical truths, consider a mental image of the spirit-soul relationship. Imagine you are in a large, darkened storehouse. This storehouse is your soul, and it holds all your earthly life experiences in the form of boxes. You navigate this darkened storehouse with a flashlight. There was a time when the storehouse was almost empty, and you were simply there with your flashlight. It took a while to figure out what was going on; however, as the storehouse gradually filled with boxes, you began to organize the world around you and your unique relationship with that world to form a unique identity. The storehouse has large glass windows for walls. Outside the storehouse, just past the windows, there are boxes representing all possible earthly life relationships. As you interact with the outside world, the relationships you form are brought into the storehouse and represented by clusters of boxes. You cannot illuminate the whole storehouse, only clusters of boxes. You can go to that location where you have stored relationships from dinner the past evening. You can go the location where you have stored the relationships from your last day of work or the last interactions you had with a friend. Certain areas of the storehouse, representing the good times in life, are visited frequently and often bring on a smile. Other areas of the storehouse tend to be avoided because they represent difficult times. Some sections of the storehouse are neat and orderly; other areas are a disastrous disorder. It is much more pleasant to visit the former than the latter. There are empty areas you visit frequently. While nothing is stored in such an area, you go there nevertheless and ponder what you will store there someday. These empty areas represent your desires, dreams and aspirations.

Getting boxes into your storehouse is as easy as engaging the outside world. You simply go to the area where experiences of that interaction are stored, shine your light through the boxes representing those experiences and out through the window into the outside world. The current interaction builds new experiences and brings them into the storehouse. Now there are two ways to bring new boxes into the storehouse. One way is easy, with the only guide being to interact in a way that seems to make sense to you or meets your immediate needs. You have discovered that this impulsive method often creates those disaster areas in your storehouse that you prefer not to visit. There is a storehouse guidebook, God's Word, available, and if the included directives are followed, the resulting interactions lead to respectable, well-organized clusters of boxes in the storehouse. The guidebook even provides instruction in dealing with messes previously made. Using the guide to bring in new boxes or reorganize previously stored boxes takes effort. The result, however, is that you can walk through your storehouse, the whole storehouse, and feel a sense of contentment and peace knowing that you are following the directives of the guidebook and getting your storehouse in order. The spirit illuminates and navigates the soul, reflects on the past, actively builds relationships in the present and ponders and plans the future.

Harmonizing

So then, the proposed taxonomy is that reasoned, purposeful behavior progresses from the heart to the spirit to the soul and that the spirit-soul interaction is referred to as the mind. If we examine Scripture, in an effort to validate the taxonomy, we discover a modification to our taxonomy is warranted. While our initial taxonomy flows from heart to spirit to soul, Scripture supports a taxonomy that flows from heart to soul to mind (spirit-soul interaction). Because we are examining the theological constructs in the context of reasoned, purposeful behavior that distinguishes man from animal, we will pursue the theme of faith in Scripture to further investigate our taxonomy. Faith has much in common with reasoned, purposeful behavior. Brown (1986) states that, "Faith is dynamic movement which requires adjustment and readjustment. Faith is bound up with making critical judgment. The fact that the gospel finds its ultimate expression and foundation in the cross of Christ means that faith must constantly measure itself by the norm" (v. 1, p. 602). Faith is not impulsive (the soul acting alone). Faith is reasoned, purposeful behavior (spirit-soul interaction). A saving faith, which is a simple, yet sufficient expression of faith, relies on reasoning. A saving faith requires that one believe and trust. There is cognitive appraisal and a behavioral expression. Peter provides us with a word picture of a mature, developing faith when he writes we are to "add to your faith goodness; and to goodness, knowledge; and to knowledge, self-control; and to self-control, perseverance..." (2 Peter 1:5-6). If we lay this progression of a maturing faith alongside our taxonomy, the similarities become obvious. Goodness is of the heart, knowledge is of the soul, self-control is a function of the mind (spirit-soul interaction) and perseverance is a new construct to be considered. While this challenges our original taxonomy by placing the soul before the spirit-soul interaction, it makes sense because the spirit needs information from the soul before it can exercise agency. Another example comes from Jesus concerning faith. Jesus reiterates the Old Testament command to "Love the Lord your God with all your heart and with all your soul and with all your mind and with all your strength" (Mark

12:30). Once again we have reasoned, purposeful behavior flowing from the heart to the soul to the mind (spirit-soul interaction). Jesus also adds strength to the end, which is similar to the concept of perseverance added by Peter.

Perseverance / Strength

Research in psychology (Festinger, 1957) supports the idea that engaging in a behavior influences one's attitude. This would indicate that persevering in a behavior would influence the attitude of one's heart. Jeeves (2002) writes, "If social psychology has taught us anything over the last 30 years, it is that we are as likely to act ourselves into a way of thinking, as to think ourselves into a way of acting... It is now a fundamental rule of social psychology that behavior and attitude generate one another in an endless spiral" (p. 7). So then, faith manifests itself in action and is further strengthened by that action, or, as Calvin (1559) put it, "Faith is born of obedience" (p. 72). Faith comes by hearing the Word of God and the Word of God must penetrate all the way to the heart. The Word of God is heard (knowledge/soul), acted on (self-control and perseverance/mind), and consequently develops goodness and virtue (heart). It is perseverance that makes one "mature and complete, lacking in nothing" (see James 1:4). Unfortunately, this process, where engaging in behavior changes your heart works both ways. Social psychologists have demonstrated that research subjects who are asked to engage in a morally wrong behavior (i.e., lying, cheating) with the rationale that it is being done for the sake of scientific data, experience a decline in their overall moral values.

The Traditional Christian View

Conservative Christian theology typically views the human spirit and soul as the same in substance and essence. This position developed in defense against heretical tri-partite teachings and continues today primarily as a defense against some Charismatic teachings that take liberties with the concept of the human spirit. Hodge (2003) provides a concise summary of the development of this conservative Christian view.

> This doctrine of a threefold constitution of man being adopted by Plato, was introduced partially into the early Church, but soon came to be regarded as dangerous, if not heretical. It's being held by the Gnostics that the pneuma in man was a part of the divine essence, and incapable of sin; and by the Apollinarians that Christ had only a human soma and psuche, but not a human pneuma, the Church rejected the doctrine that the psuche and pneuma were distinct substances, since upon it those heresies were founded. In later times the Semi-Pelagians taught that the soul and body, but not the spirit in man, were the subjects of original sin. All Protestants, Lutherans and Reformed, were, therefore, the more zealous in maintaining that the soul and spirit, psuche and pneuma, are one and the same substance and essence. And this, as before remarked, has been the common doctrine of the church." (p. 53)

Many theologians state that the spirit and soul (and even the heart and mind) are fundamentally the same because there are some examples in Scripture where each term is used to refer to the whole of man. I propose that it is common to use a single term for emphasis while implying more. We will revisit our chariot analogy to illustrate. Suppose you were going to the chariot races in Athens. You might phrase an invitation to another based on your specific area of interest. If you are most interested in watching the muscular and powerful team of horses that pull the chariot and represent the soul you might say, "Let's go watch the teams race." If your interest lies in showing loyalty to the home team that represents the heart you might say, "Let's go watch the Athenians race." If you enjoy watching the charioteers, who represent the spirit, skillfully control the team of horses you might say, "Let's go watch the charioteers race." And finally, if you were interested in the whole of the sport, representing the whole of man, you might say, "Let's go watch the chariots race."

I find it incongruent when a theologian writes that the spirit is immaterial and the soul is material, the spirit is what man has in common with God and the soul is what man has in common with animals and then proceeds to assign different characteristics to each only to conclude that the spirit and soul are the same in substance and in essence. If, as Hodge (2003) states, this was done to protect against misuse of the concepts, are we not trading one fallacy for another? I think it would be much more productive to focus our attention, more specifically, to the duality of the immaterial spirit and the material soul (at least that part of the soul man has in common with animals). There are numerous questions that need to be addressed. How do an immaterial spirit and a material soul interact? Where is the line of demarcation between the spirit and soul and can it be identified? How does the immaterial spirit function when the material soul has been functionally impaired (i.e., trauma, dementia and Alzheimer's disease)? And the big one, how does a material soul survive death? Concerning this final question I see three possible answers. One, God just makes it happen. Two, there is an immaterial component to the material soul. Finally, through a type if symbiosis or transference the heart/spirit acquires characteristics of personhood from the soul. When the material soul dies, the heart/spirit are purified (purged from any corruption) and the most important components of personhood are conserved through the eternal heart/spirit. For humans, which are both spiritual and material, Scripture attaches the concept of personhood to the material soul. On the other hand, angels are spirits and they possess personhood, as does God. Consider this example. When you first meet someone they occupy a place in your material soul. They are a collection of data points stored in the physical brain. As you come to know the person better they begin occupy a place much deeper in your being. When I first met my wife she was represented by data in my material soul - and I liked that data. As I came to know her better and interacted with her at a more personal level, she began to be represented much deeper in my being. Now, after more than thirty years, she not only occupies a large part of my soul, she occupies a large part of my heart. Let's revisit our chariot analogy one last time to clarify this proposition. You can take away a well-seasoned charioteer's horses and chariot but he will always be an Athenian Charioteer!

CHAPTER 3

DEFINING THE SOUL

Defining the Soul

We now begin an exploration toward defining the human soul, or, what we often refer to as personhood in humans. There is a place, or maybe "perspective" would be more accurate, of understanding where I want to take the reader. I choose an introspective approach, because engaging the self will lead to a more personal experience. Imagine that I were to ask you to write an autobiography. In essence, then, with pen and paper you would bare your soul. I would encourage you to be honest and objective because only you will analyze the document. Now, reader, stop reading this book and take a few minutes to consider the information with which you would begin your autobiography and then what you would include from your life to the present. Once you have thought about that for a few minutes, proceed with your reading.

Now we can analyze what you found relevant to include in your definition of self and see if we can learn something regarding what defines your soul. We can probably separate your document into three distinct periods of life. The first period of life, or maybe more of a point in time, that defines your soul would be birth information. These first defining characteristics were given to you by your parents and form the starting point of your existence. Birth information includes your name, place of birth, and date of birth. These are fundamental identifiers of self. My family moved from my birth state when I was very young, yet, I'll always be a Texan. The year 1958 holds a special place in my heart, and my name is, well, my name. Specific circumstances may have prompted you to begin your story before or after birth. Some may have begun before birth, if a major event occurred while your mother carried you *in utero*. Maybe your mother was considering an abortion and then changed her mind at the last minute, and you learned of this and it became part of your personhood. If you were adopted at a very early age, you may not know your place of birth or your first given name, and you may be forced to begin at the adoption. Other circumstances one was born into can also be defining characteristics of the soul. A person born during the Great Depression identifies with hard times. A child born when his or her father was off to war sees that fact as important to personhood. John the Baptist jumped in the womb of his mother Elizabeth when she saw Mary with child (see Luke 1:41); Jacob was born grasping Esau's heel (see Genesis 25:26); and Jesus was born in a stable (see Luke 2:7). Surely these events, even though there was no personal awareness of them at the time, were passed down verbally and became a part of the personhood of each of these individuals. Wherever you began and whatever you wrote, each truth is a piece of you and a part of the definition of your soul.

The second period of life would include early childhood wherein your self is defined primarily through your relationship with parents. Inclusions during the first few years of life tend to focus more on the lives of parents and family, and your self is defined through them to a large degree. You might write of the economic status of your family, the type of neighborhood you lived in or your parent's occupation. Where and how often your parents went to church and their level of spiritual maturity might be discussed. Extended family members would be mentioned if they were relevant to your early years of life. You also might include any major events that affected your family even though you do not really have any personal recollection. Because most people do not recall much, if anything, from the very early years of life, they are forced to fill in their identity of self through family knowledge. At the end of this period, as you move into the third period, you begin to have recollections that stand out as uniquely yours. Those who recall them more vividly typically embellish memories of these events. I recall–maybe embellished to some degree by my father's account–seeing John F. Kennedy the day before Lee Harvey Oswald assassinated him. I also remember shaking Vice President Lyndon B. Johnson's hand at my father's request. Dad said, "Shake this man's hand, Jay–he'll be President of the United States some day." I also vaguely remember the Vice President's wife sitting down next to my mother and talking with her. I am certain I recall someone calling the Vice President's wife "Ladybird" and wondering why she did not take offense to that title. I do not know which of those events I actually remember and which ones were inserted into my memory through discussions among family members over the years. I do know that those events became a small part of my life and, therefore, a part of my soul.

Now we'll continue with your autobiography. As you move further into this third period of your life, you begin to notice how conscious choices began to shape the definition of your soul. Here you include your choice of friends throughout the years; you include major life transitions including educational and occupational changes and how you handled them. You include events that may or may not have been within your control that had a major impact on your identity. You did, however, have a choice in how you perceived those events and some control over how the events shaped your life. Maybe your parents had to move to another state, and you were separated from your friends. An event like this can be very difficult for any child, and the outcome depends, to a large degree, on the child's willingness to adjust to the new circumstances. Since we are most interested in developing an understanding of what defines the soul in the context of the present, this final period will be the object of our focus.

To summarize, during the early years of life, a child's identity is formed through his or her parents. During the teen years, there is a drive toward autonomy, and the child resists the earlier parent-imposed definition and attempts to identify self apart from parents. This sometimes-tumultuous period is often marked by extreme highs and lows of emotion and is often referred to as "the best of times and the worst of times." Gradually, the autonomous self is formed, and the individual becomes responsible for actions and reactions to life events.

The Soul is Defined by Relationships

Now that we have a good idea of what you might include in defining your soul, we can subject this document to a final analysis. What we are looking for is an answer to a single question: What do all those defining experiences, recorded in your autobiography, have in common? Ponder that for a moment. What is the common thread woven through those dates, names, places, people and events, along with their associated thoughts and emotions? The answer is that you have developed a relationship with all of those things that define your personhood. Those dates, names, places and people all exist (or can exist) on their own, in and of themselves. What is relevant is that somewhere in time each has related to you in a personal way and become part of your life, your self, the definition of your individual soul. Indeed, you are defined by your relationships and your specific collection of relationships is unique to you. Two people may respond differently to the same event simply because that event is perceived in the context of each individual's soul relationships.

The fact that you are defined by your relationships helps us see why each event in your life must be viewed in the context of your whole life. Each new relationship is shaped in some way by previous relationships. When I worked at the psychiatric hospital, we had a large number of schizophrenic patients who experienced delusions of grandeur. Some of these patients had assumed grandiose identities. One group of patients assumed identities of biblical characters. At one point, there were three patients who claimed to be Jesus and two of those patients were females. Of course, each accused the other two of being the anti-Christ. Two other patients had assumed the biblical identities of Mary and Abraham. Another group of patients had chosen to manifest their grandiose delusions by assuming the identities of either superheroes, or famous, secular historical characters. A young man thought he was Superman and two older patients claimed to be Abraham Lincoln and Joan of Arc. As I pondered on their choices, and thinking that you can't get more grandiose than Jesus or at least a biblical character, I systematically worked my way through each of the patients case histories. What I discovered was that there were notations in the case histories to religious affiliation and evidence that religion had been an influence in the lives of those patients who chose to assume the identities of biblical characters. Those patients who claimed to be superheroes or famous historical figures had no religious affiliation and no references to religion in their case histories. As they say, you can't paint with colors you don't have, or, each new event in your life must be viewed in the context of your whole life.

Maybe an analogy would be helpful at this point. Many words in the English language have more than one meaning. One way to discover the meaning intended for a word in a given situation is to view it in the context of other words, a sentence. Words are defined by their relationships to other words; sentences are best understood in the context of paragraphs. Some words take on new meanings by being related to new words. The result is that new definitions are added to specific words in dictionaries because words have become redefined by their new relationships. Words, as must people, need to be defined in their context.

Let us briefly examine the idea that the soul is defined by its relationships from a few other perspectives. As mentioned earlier, psychology has generated many theories of psychotherapy that attempt to define, and ultimately redefine, the soul. Additionally, we acknowledge that these theories fall short in their quest because they were structured on faulty presuppositions and fail to fully engage the spiritual component within man. Even so, there are interesting characteristics that these theories have in common. One of those characteristics is that every viable theory of psychotherapy incorporates into its structure for defining and redefining the soul the importance of relationships. Some theories focus on a broad range of interpersonal relationships while others tend to sharpen the focus to significant others, family members or relationships through which problems originated. Other theories focus on the congruence or incongruence of the self-relationship. Even our understanding of the physiology of the human brain supports the idea that man was created to function through relationships. Cognitive psychologists tell us that we organize information in our brain through association. These elaborate associations are referred to as schemas, representing the complex associations and interrelatedness in the context of a whole. Cognitive schemas are fluid, constantly changing. These changes occur as new associations, or relationships, are formed through new life experiences.

Finally, we can look to the actual physical structure in the brain that is responsible for organizing and maintaining our experiences. The brain contains elongated cells called neurons that transmit information to other neurons along neural pathways. These pathways are the location wherein information from associations or relationships is stored. The human brain has approximately one hundred billion neurons and each neuron has approximately seven thousand connections to other neurons. The number of connections in the human brain outnumbers the number of connections in the Internet by an astronomical number. Scientists believe that the human brain has the storage capacity to remember every experience that has come through the senses, along with the pieces of information generated by the person reflecting on these experiences. Data from each individual experience is likely stored in multiple locations, and the storage process is fluid, changing with successive relationships. Research in neuroscience has demonstrated that new experiences, that can include but are not limited to new knowledge, thoughts and behaviors, travel down naïve or inexperienced neural pathways. As one continues to engage in a new association, or when a single association is salient, the neurons actually develop new growth that results in new, more efficient neural pathways. Researchers in neuroscience can actually demonstrate these neurological changes that take place, over a number of trials, with two live neurons in a Petri dish. Neuroscientists have developed a saying, "Neurons that fire together, wire together." So new firing causes new wiring, or new relationships create a new definition of self.

When a violinist discovers that a new set of finger positions on the strings is difficult, it is due to the fact that the violinist is using pre-existing neural pathways that are not well equipped to deal with the novel behavior. As the violinist continues to practice difficult finger positions on the strings they become less difficult as naïve neural pathways go through their learning process. Continued practice moves the neural activity from the inefficient pre-existing neural pathways to the newly educated pathways created specifically for the new finger positions. This has the desired effect of taking the finger positions from difficult, to less difficult to second nature.

Research on human memory has demonstrated that engaging a new stimulus three times may be the most efficient means of making it permanent (see Ebbinghaus, 1885/1962; Jost, 1897; Boneau, 1998). Furthermore, taking a break, referred to as the "incubation effect," followed by a reengagement of the new stimulus with three more repetitions is the most efficient means of enhancing the new learning. Three repetitions work better than one, or two and three repetitions work better than four or more up to twelve repetitions. So three repetitions appear to be the optimal number of repetitions necessary to create a new neural pathway. What neurological changes did

Peter experience when he denied Jesus, not once, but three times (see Matthew 26:75)? How did the repetition impact the definition of his soul? And again, what neurological changes did Peter experience when given the opportunity to affirm his love for Jesus, not once, but three times (see John 21:15-17)? Could it be that it took three repetitions of denial for Peter to experience the formation of new neural pathways, thereby confirming his weakness? And could it be that it took three repetitions of his affirmation of his love for Jesus to experience the formation of new neural pathways, thereby confirming his renewed devotion to Jesus? There is a qualitative neurological change that occurs when a stimulus is engaged a single time and there is a quantitative neurological change that occurs when a stimulus is engaged multiple times. Another distinction worth noting is that the potential for a new relationship is not the same as actually forming a new relationship. Being omniscient, God knew that Abraham would be willing to offer his son Isaac as a sacrifice. It was the act of faith, the actual engagement in the salient behavior that fired and educated once naïve neural pathways and redefined Abraham's soul as faithful (see James 2:21-23). By demonstrating his faith in God and engaging in a new relationship Abraham became a man of great faith. What Abraham became, positioned him to be the father of God's chosen people (see Genesis 12:1-3) and, indeed, all believers (see Romans 4:11).

It is important here to understand that the world in which one lives, the one where most relationships originally form, is internally represented in the human soul. Consider this example. The Word of God is printed on pages within the binding of a book that sits on a shelf. God's Holy Word, as powerful and important as it is, exists on its own apart from a person and has no effect on the soul of an individual. However, if the person picks up that book, opens it and reads the words on its pages, he or she has then related to the Word of God. The Word of God is represented internally and, to the degree that it is engaged, becomes a very real part of their selfhood. The more one reads God's Word, the more he or she relates to God's Word and the more pronounced the change within the human soul. Think of the people whom you have known who have died. You will readily accept that some of those people, even though they are no longer present, continue to have a profound impact on your personhood. That is because those relationships you formed through experience with these people are represented internally. Though no longer present, those people shaped who you are and–through memories–may mold the person you will become.

Finally, we examine Scripture and the Christian tradition for evidence to support the idea that the human soul is defined by relationships. Theologians attribute the relational quality of man to his being created in the image of God. Cottrell (2002) states that capacity for intellect, language, volition, morality, creativity and emotions "find their full expression in human beings in that each can be employed spiritually in the course of one's relationship with God" (pp. 152,153). Kirwan (1984) states, "The Bible speaks of covenants, commandments, doctrines, sins, and holiness. All of these concepts imply some sort of relationship–a vertical relationship between God and humans, a horizontal relationship between humans, or perhaps both. Yet these concepts are often discussed as if they were entities unto themselves, as if they had nothing to do with relationships" (p. 81). Roberts & Talbot (1997) note the need for interpersonal relationships and stewardship in a discussion of the basic teleology of human nature:

> The Bible emphasizes three basic directions of human nature: the need to honor, serve, and depend on God

> as Father; the need to stand in a relationship of mutual dependency and harmony with other human beings; and the need to take care of the creation. Thus, human nature is basically "relational," our well-being depending on relationships with God, our human fellows, and the natural world that befit the nature of each of these. (p. 77)

Created in the image of God, man is relational. For man to function as he was created, the proper relationships need to exist. If the proper relationships do not exist, man will not function as his Creator intended. An understanding that a soul is defined by its relationships becomes necessary in the context of redefining the soul of an individual. Basically, the human soul can develop in relationship toward God or away from God. A soul that develops toward God will be growing in proper relation to Him and His will. In contrast, a soul that develops away from God will be in growing in relation to the world and the things of the world. Therefore, man has only two choices: to grow toward God and develop the spiritual self, or to grow away from God and develop the worldly self. This battle between righteousness and evil is waged within each of us. Will we love our Creator and relate to His creation as He intended, or will we love the world and forsake our Creator?

To this point, we understand that the soul is defined by relationships. These soul-defining relationships will either grow toward the will of God or away from the will of God. The interaction of the spirit-soul relation makes it possible to evaluate past relationships and choose a new direction with new relationships. In the next chapter, we will identify and label the soul-defining relationships, explore the relationships between those relationships, and we will discover, thereby, the parameters of the human soul.

CHAPTER 4

PARAMETERS OF THE SOUL

Parameters of the Soul

We now begin the quest of identifying the parameters of the human soul. We know that Scripture uses the term soul in reference to that part of man that is formed by earthly life experiences, what we are calling relationships. We also know that Scripture tells us the spirit of man knows his thoughts and searches his innermost parts. The spirit-soul relation allows man to actively interact with the outside world and to exercise some control in choosing specific relationships that will potentially define him and how he relates to, or perceives those experiences. Man can make a conscious decision to build relationships that bring him closer to the will of God or alienate him from God. As we begin to contemplate the parameters of the soul, we acknowledge that man's free will must be taken into consideration. Free will dictates that the relationships that form the parameters of the soul would include more than the relationships that define any single, individual soul. Our focus must shift from actual relationships represented by a specific human soul to all possible relationships that could potentially define that human soul. (See figure 4-1.) While that appears to be a daunting task, it will be manageable if we reduce the number of possible relationships to their simplest form.

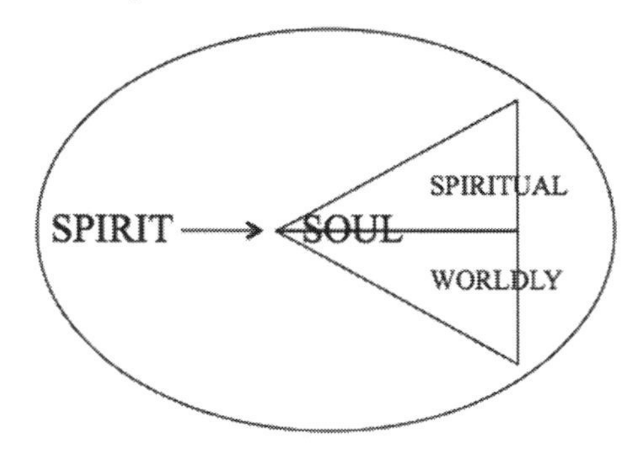

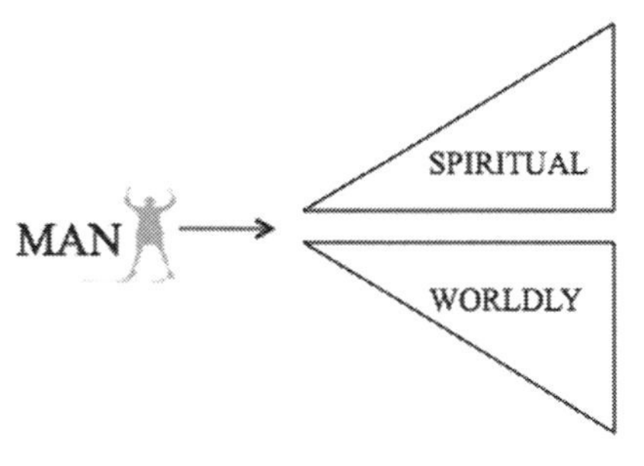

Figure 4-1

In its simplest form, all possible relationships are as follows. Man can have a positive relationship to God and His creation, or man can have a negative relationship to

God and His creation. There are no other options - no multiple choices. Scripture reveals that we live and function in a world of spiritual alternatives. We can live by faith or by sight (see 2 Corinthians 5:7). We can be children of light or darkness (see Ephesians 5:8). We can follow the straight and narrow or the crooked and perverse (see Proverbs 28:18). We can build our house on the rock or on the sand (see Matthew 7:24-27). We can practice the wisdom from above or the wisdom from below (see James 3:15-17). Or, as Jesus said, "He who is not with me is against me" (Matthew 12:30a). Speaking broadly about all possible relationships, we must acknowledge the choices are not multiple; the choices are two.

Now, one might begin to think that it is possible, even probable, that some people have neither a positive or negative relationship with God. Is it not possible that there are people who have no relationship with God? The answer is "No." Scripture affirms that every man has the evidence of God available to him through God's creation (see Psalms 19:1; Acts 14:17; Romans 1:19, 20). Additionally, God has planted the knowledge of Himself in the heart of man (see Romans 1:26-32; 2:14, 15). As Cottrell (2002) states, "The result of this general revelation is that all normal adults have a true knowledge of God as Creator, Ruler, and Lawgiver, and a true knowledge of his basic will for his human creatures. To deny God and flout his law in the face of general revelation is an act of will, a suppression of known truth" (p. 45). God is man's Creator, and God has made Himself known through direct and general revelation to all man. As a result, man can have a positive relationship with God or a negative relationship with God. A negative relationship with God indicates a positive relationship with the world, for "no one can serve two masters. Either he will hate the one and love the other, or he will be devoted to the one and despise the other"

(Matthew 6:24). Conversely, a positive relationship with God indicates a negative relationship with the world. There are no multiple choices, only alternatives.

The alternatives are clear. Man can either relate to God and His creation in a manner that is congruent with God's will (positive relationship), or man can have a negative relationship with God and relate to God's creation in ways that displease God. Therefore, the soul will develop toward God and His will or away from God and toward the world.

The Spiritual Triad

We begin our exploration of the parameters of the soul with God's intended relationships. Man was created to have a relationship with God and a purpose within the context of God's creation (see Genesis 1 and 2). God facilitates this relationship by specifying His purpose, or directives, for man through His Word. These expectations constitute the goals of the God-man relationship and fall under the precepts of His commandments (see Matthew 19:17), His will for our lives (see Hebrews 10:36), the fruit of the Spirit that Christians are to produce (see Galatians 5:22), or simply the new-man, new-self or regenerated soul (see Ephesians 4:24). We strive for a harmonious relationship with God, and through this harmonious relationship we discover how to relate correctly to His creation.

When we diagram God's intended relationships, we discover something interesting. What we discover about the relationships between God, man, and His directives (goals) for relating to His creation is that the relationships have names. (See figure 4-2.)

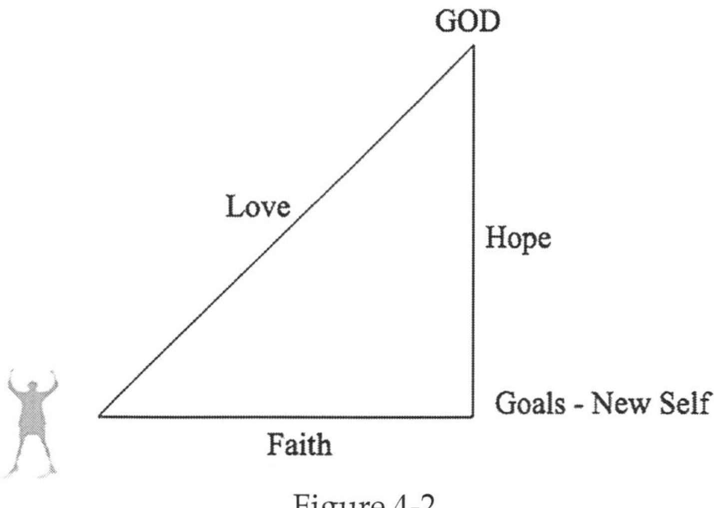

Figure 4-2

The relationship between God and man is a love relationship. God loved us before the foundation of the earth (see Ephesians 1:4), and He demonstrated His love for us, while we were still sinners, through the death of His Son (see Romans 5:8). The relationship between God and His directives for our lives is hope. It is the new self, the self formed by building a relationship, by faith, with the will of God that finds grace, holiness, and hope (see Ephesians 4:24). Finally, the relationship between man and God's will for man's life is faith. Man's work (fruit of the Spirit or New Self) is produced by faith (see 1 Thessalonians 1:3), and only by faith do we have access to our inheritance, our hope (see Hebrews 6:12). The relationships among these three relationships are firmly established in God's Word. Through the Word of God we discover that of the three, love is the greatest (see 1 Corinthians 13:13), that "faith and love . . . spring from the hope that is stored up for you in heaven" (Colossians 1:5), that work is produced by faith, labor is prompted by love, and endurance is inspired by hope (see 1 Thessalonians 1:3), and that the armor of God includes faith and love as a breastplate and also includes the hope of our salvation as a helmet (see 1 Thessalonians 5:8). The spiritual triad, the way God wants man to function, includes the components of man, God, and His creation bound by the relationships of faith, hope, and love.

One passage of Scripture paints a simple, yet beautiful, word picture of the spiritual relationship triad. David wrote in Psalms 139:9, 10, "If I rise on the wings of the dawn, if I settle on the far side of the sea, even there your hand will guide me, your right hand will hold me fast." Picture this passage in your mind by imagining you are standing on the sharp, slippery rocks of life at the edge of a raging sea. The waves are violently crashing onto the slippery rocks with the sole purpose of engulfing and devouring you. You're paralyzed by fear and unable to move. Which way to go? Any step could be fatal. It is hard to take your eyes off the sea; yet, your eyes frantically search for an escape. When your eyes look upward, you discover that God has reached down with His right hand in love and He has been holding you securely. You then look ahead, out past the treacherous rocks and see the other hand of God, pointing the way, offering hope, guiding you to safety. Will you have faith in Him? Will you go where He leads?

The Worldly Triad

It would be wonderful if this were the complete picture: loved by God, living by faith, and secure in the hope that comes down from the glory of God. Of course, the problem is that there is another who desires to build a relationship with man. Satan, the great deceiver, the father of lies, and the prince of this world, desperately desires to come into relation with man – to destroy him. This means additional relationships must be introduced into our relationships that can potentially define the soul.

The Satan-man relationship is a distorted inversion of the God-man relationship. The God-man relationship is spiritual and assumes a proper position on top. The Satan-man relationship is worldly and, therefore, assumes a lower position. I picture the Satan-man relationship lines as faded or wavy to signify that they are a distorted reflection of the perfected relationships God desires to have with man. Satan's relationships are like shifting shadows, shadows of the solid, substantive God-man relationship (see James 1:17). Satan builds relationships through deception because he has no choice, for if man saw Satan as he really is, Satan could build a relationship with no one. For this reason, "Satan himself masquerades as an angel of light" (2 Corinthians 11:14). Satan attempts to get a person [you!] to build a relationship with him and creation in ways that are grounded in him. Relating to God's creation in a worldly way is what the Bible calls living by sight (see 2 Corinthians 5:7), the acts of the sinful nature (see Galatians 5:19), or the old self (see Ephesians 4:22). These relationships cannot be the same as faith, hope, and love. Instead they are a distorted reflection, a corruption, of faith, hope, and love. So what are Biblical terms for these relationships? If the foundational quality of the God-man relationship is love, what will it be for the Satan-man relationship? Of course, the opposite of love, hate, is the first thing that springs to mind. But there are two problems with hate as the opposite. First, the Bible does not support that as a tie between Satan and man, and second, one cannot imagine a person would be tempted to build a positive relationship with anyone based on hate. So it must be the other opposite of love: self-love. Godly love focuses externally on the needs of others; self-love focuses internally (see Romans 2:8). Now let's examine the relationship we can have to creation when we ground it in our relationship with the world. God desires us to build a relationship with His creation through faith in His directives. Satan offers up things of the world to relate to, not by faith, but by sight. Finally, God offers hope and life to those who live by faith. In contrast, all Satan has to offer is hopelessness and death. He desperately desires that by the time one realizes the hopelessness of associating with him, it will be too late. Let's diagram these relationships for a visualization of the alternatives available to man. (See figure 4-3.)

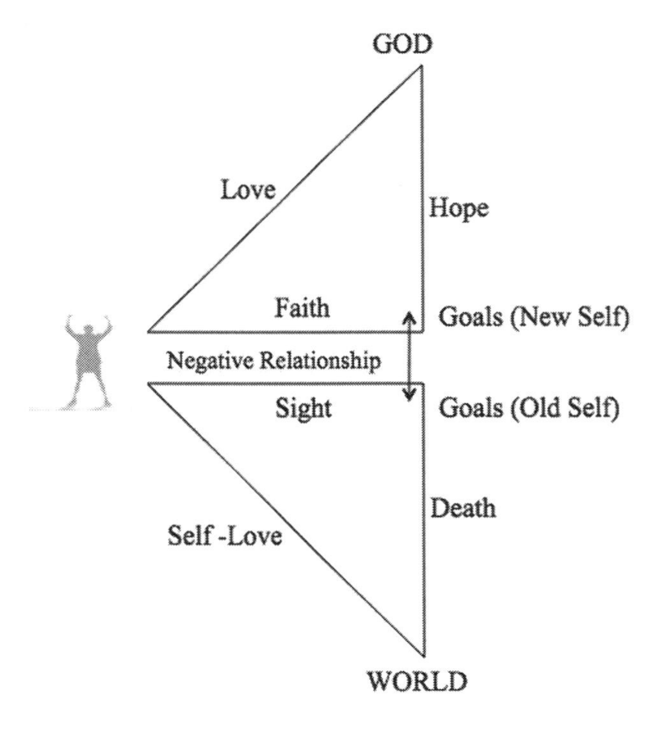

Figure 4-3

The Seven Soul Defining Relationships

We have arrived at six of the seven relationships that define the soul. Three relationships correspond to the spiritual realm (love/faith/hope and life), and three relationships correspond to the earthly/worldly realm (self-love/sight/hopelessness and death). The seventh relationship springs forth from the worldly triad and is very real. It is represented by the relationship between the new self and the old self, between righteousness and sin, between the spiritual and worldly triads. This relationship is always negative and even necessary given man's fallen state. The relationship is always negative because the spiritual and worldly triads are always in disagreement with one another. The negative relationship is necessary because it allows discernment to be possible. The apostle Paul stated that he would not be able to identify sin if it were not for knowing righteousness (see Romans 3:20). The negative is based on the Scriptural precedent that man cannot serve two masters. The relationship is negative in that light cannot fellowship with darkness (see 2 Corinthians 6:14), and freshwater and saltwater cannot flow from the same spring (see James 3:11). The implications of this negative relationship will become more evident when we explore what Scripture says about dealing with temptation. Consequently, we have seven possible relationships, three representing the spiritual realm and four representing the earthly realm. As you consider these seven relationships, you will conclude, as I have, that they are complete. These seven relationships define the dimensions of human existence, the parameters of one's soul. That may be a bold statement; yet, I believe it is a valid one.

The Seven Cardinal Virtues

It is interesting to note that the cohesiveness of these seven soul-defining relationships have already been identified by man, to an extent. Plato held that the four virtues of temperance, prudence, fortitude, and justice were the highest moral virtues attainable. He believed that these four virtues corresponded to the natural constitution of the human soul and were achievable through human effort alone. Temperance (man-world relationship; self-love) as a virtue moderated man's ongoing sensual relationship with the world and encouraged restraint in the fulfilling of physical appetites. Prudence (man-old self relationship; sight) encouraged restraint in relationships that were chosen by will and focused on obtaining relevant knowledge and making ethical decisions based on the information available. Fortitude (world-old self relationship; hopelessness and death) addressed man's ability to muster courage when faced with hopeless situations of danger and even death. Each of these virtues ultimately focused inwardly (self-serving) on the individual to lead to a higher level of moral functioning. The fourth virtue, justice, bridged the gap between the worldly and spiritual triads and attempted to shift the focus externally toward one's fellow man as it attempted to moderate between selfishness and selflessness. Justice was a personal attempt to treat others, as you would want to be treated. Aristotle continued to develop Plato's teachings on the virtues. Due to the salient practices of favoritism in his era, Aristotle became disenchanted with the virtue of justice believing it to be an unattainable virtue for the average man. He concluded that only when all the virtues were lived at their purest level could the possibility for a true justice exist. As Aristotle (Magn. moral) said, "In justice is all virtue involved." Four hundred years later, Paul introduced the three theological or spiritual virtues of faith, hope, and love (see 1 Corinthians 13:13). The three theological virtues are selfless and are possible only through a sanctifying grace. In other words, the only way one can truly express Christian faith, hope, and love is supernaturally through the work of Christ on the cross and the indwelling of the Holy Spirit. (See figure 4-4.) What Aristotle had longed for, "a higher standing-point where justice passes into love" had been realized through Jesus Christ and Aristotle was prophetically correct when he said, "there is no need for justice where love is present" (Neander, 1853). I am certain Aristotle could not have comprehended the love that was to come through One called Jesus. For it was not justice that Jesus introduced, but grace and forgiveness. It is worthwhile to note that these seven virtues together are referred to as "cardinal" (Latin: *cardo*, meaning *hinge*) virtues. Therefore, every human virtue in some way hinges on one or another of these seven virtues. In other words, they are seven fundamental virtues that define the parameters of the soul.

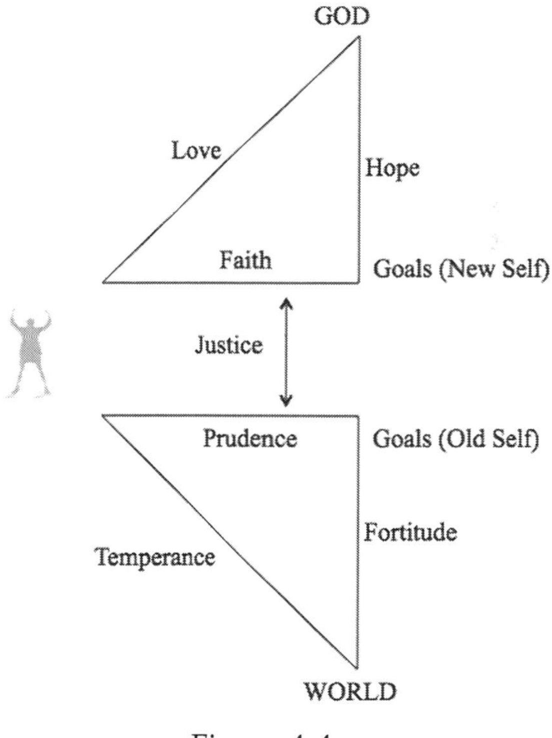

Figure 4-4

The Spiritual Triad—Ties that Bind

Ecclesiastes 4:12 declares, "A cord of three strands is not easily broken." So it is with the God-man relationship. We have discovered that love–godly love that focuses on us to meet our needs–is a most important tie that binds God to Man. We know that God loved us before the foundation of the world (see Ephesians 1:4) and that nothing can separate us from the love of God (see Romans 8:39). It is this love that motivates us to live a life of faith. God's love compels us to follow Him as recipient and to serve Him as facilitators of His Word (see 2 Corinthians 5:14). Scripture guides us into an understanding that love is only one of three strands that binds God to man. The second tie that binds God to man is the Word of Truth. Without the Word of Truth, we would not know about the love of God. Additionally, only through the Word can we discover His will for our lives, the precepts (goals) of God for man. The Word dwells in our hearts and provides our direction. The Word is a lamp to our feet and a light to our path (see Psalms 119:105), and the Word of Truth is the only source of faith mentioned in Scripture (see Romans 10:17). The third tie that binds God and man is the Holy Spirit. The Holy Spirit works on unregenerate man to convict him of his fallen state. Once we give our lives to God, the Holy Spirit works from within, testifying that we are children of God and empowering us to live by faith. At this point we are given a new name, Christian (see Romans 8:16). (See figure 4-5.) So the three strands of the relationship that binds God and man are Christian love, the Word of Truth and the Holy Spirit.

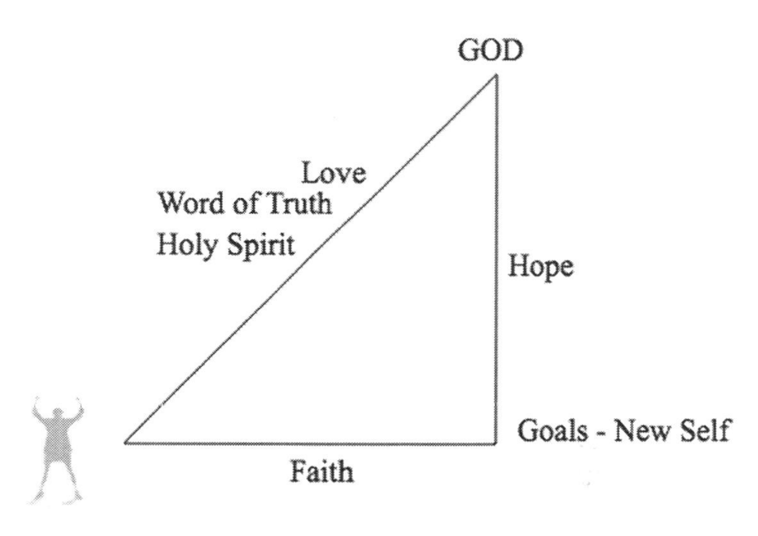

Figure 4-5

Though my wife was not a Christian when I met her, she had a special characteristic that was very attractive to me that I had not found in another woman; she liked me! Needless to say, I decided to pursue the relationship. As we got to know each other and began to date we attended church and Bible study together. During that period of our lives I witnessed a transformation in my wife to be. She had always been a good person, living a life close to the will of God, but through exposure to the Word of God the Holy Spirit convicted her of the necessity to live her life within the will of God. She gave her life to Christ and took a new name, Christian. It became obvious that her day-to-day life of faith was motivated by the awareness of Christ's love for her and the love she had for Him. As she continued to study God's Word, her thoughts, words and deeds gradually aligned more and more with the will of God. Her spirit and soul were now interacting, reasoning, in a manner consistent with a child of God. Some years later we stood in our kitchen preparing lunch and watching our two oldest daughters through the kitchen window playing on the swings in the backyard. It was obvious that my wife was deep in her thoughts when she turned to me and asked, "how does a person really know that they have the Holy Spirit?" Before I could respond with a really dumb answer she held up her finger and said, "I'll be right back" and quickly headed to the back yard to talk to some neighborhood girls that had come to play. A few minutes later she returned and I hoped that maybe she had forgotten her question. She hadn't and she repeated it. Not knowing exactly how to respond I asked her why she had gone outside. She replied, "I noticed that Sherry and Debbi were in the yard playing with our girls and I wanted to invite them to Vacation Bible School." "That's how you know you have the Holy Spirit," I replied. I've since had many students ask the same question in class. My response is always the same as I simply ask them to ponder the daily choices they make and ask themselves if they would make those same choices if they were not Christians? An immediate expression of peace is evident on their faces as they realize the Holy Spirit indeed testifies with our spirit that we are children of God (see Romans 8:16). Man is motivated by love, enabled by Truth, and empowered by the Holy Spirit to live by faith.

Take a moment to think about those three ties that bind the God-man relationship in the context of a parent-child relationship. What so strongly binds a parent and child that a parent would give up his or her life for their child? First, there is an unconditional love that is experienced by decent parents for their child. My wife and I have four children, and when our first was born, it gave me a whole new perspective on God's love for me. Once I felt how strong my love was for my child, I realized that I had nothing to worry about if God loved me half that much, and He actually loves me much, much more. That love a parent has for a child is communicated to the child in many ways on a daily basis. We call it unconditional love, and God communicates a more perfect love to us through His Word. Just as there is something special about your family name and the unity it inspires, there is a bond that springs up from wearing the name Christian.

Reading through the New Testament with this faith, hope, and love structure in mind, will validate its accuracy. While many passages of Scripture support the relationships, Romans 5:1-11 does it extraordinarily well. Read through the following passage with these relationships in mind. As you read, acknowledge that you are reading the Word of God and as such are actively in a relationship with Him. I have underlined key words or phrases.

> Therefore, since we have been justified through faith, we have peace with God through our Lord Jesus Christ, through whom we have gained access by faith into this grace in which we now stand. And we rejoice in the hope of the glory of God. Not only so, but we also rejoice in our sufferings, because we know that suffering produces perseverance; perseverance, character; and character hope. And hope does not disappoint us, because God has poured out his love into our hearts by the Holy Spirit, whom he has given us. You see, at just the right time, when we were still powerless, Christ died for the ungodly. Very rarely will anyone die for a righteous man, though for a good man someone might possibly dare to die. But God demonstrates his own love for us in this: While we were still sinners, Christ died for us. Since we have now been justified by his blood, how much more shall we be saved from God's wrath through him! For if, when we were God's enemies, we were reconciled to him through the death of his Son, how much more, having been reconciled, shall

> we be saved through his life! Not only is this so, but we also rejoice in God through our Lord Jesus Christ, through whom we have now received reconciliation.

This passage of Scripture not only supports the relationship structure we have thus far, it also provides insights to lead us to a more complete picture of this God-man relationship triad. First, the faith-hope-love relationship is possible only through Jesus Christ. It is through Jesus that we gain access by faith into the grace, which is our hope. God demonstrated His love to us by sending His Son, Jesus, to die for us while we were still sinners. As such, our faith is in Jesus. Jesus is the Word of Truth that became flesh (see John 1:14). Jesus is the way to our hope, and our hope of eternal life is in His blood shed for us. It is no wonder that the testimony of the Spirit, the water, and the blood (see 1 John 5:8) and Jesus' testimony that He is the Way and the Truth and the Life (see John 14:6) places Jesus Christ at the heart of the spiritual triad. (See figure 4-6.)

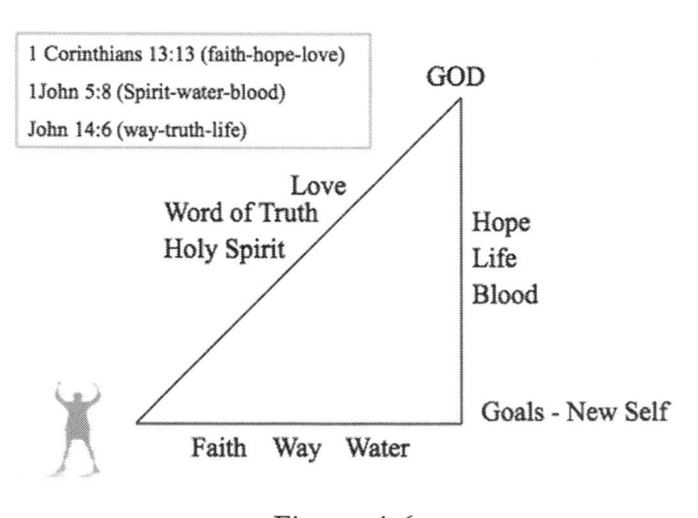

Figure 4-6

The Worldly Triad – Shadows of Ties that Bind

Once again, we discover that Satan has a counter offering for man. God intends for man to be motivated by love, enabled by Truth, and empowered by the Holy Spirit. Satan's offering is a distorted reflection of the perfect. As stated earlier, Satan attempts to motivate man through self-love. Many Christians believe that at the root of every sin is selfishness and a sound argument could be made for that statement. Regardless, all will agree that self-love is a powerful motivator. Additionally, Satan enables man through deceitful scheming (see Ephesians 4:14) and empowers his deceptions through the spirit of falsehood (see 1 John 4:6), often displaying counterfeit miracles, wonders, and signs (see 2 Thessalonians 2:9). (See figure 4-7.) The spirit of falsehood is anything that testifies on behalf of, or provides support for, the worldly deception. We hear people ask, "How can something be wrong when it feels so right?" And another person says, "That's the way I grew up," or "everyone else is doing it." I once had an international student tell me that in his country there are many false teachers and each false teacher uses some form of trickery to convince the hearer that his message is true. He said they had developed the saying, "every guru has a gimmick," from observing this relationship.

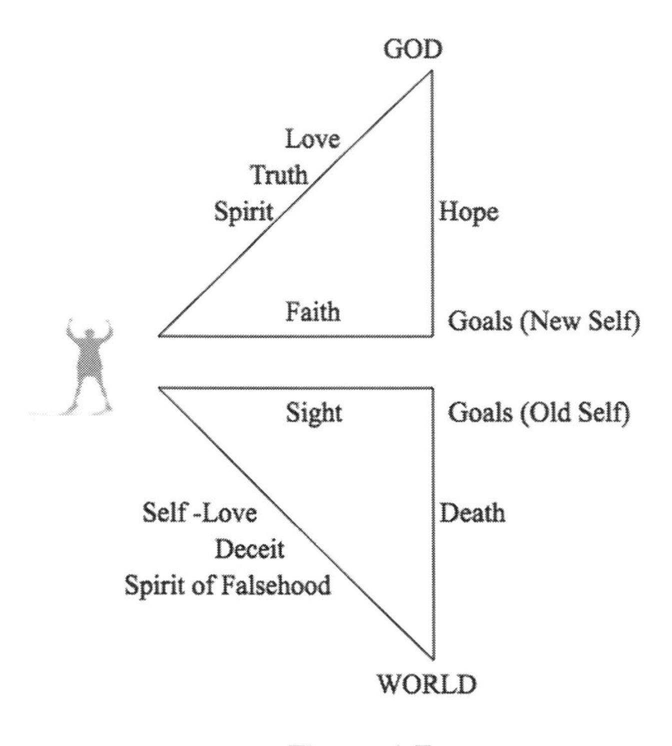

Figure 4-7

Satan is master at making nothing look like something. When I ponder the contrast between these two triads, I am reminded of an Aesop's fable called "The Dog and the Shadow."

> It happened that a Dog had got a piece of meat and was carrying it home in his mouth to eat it in peace. Now on his way home he had to cross a plank lying across a running brook. As he crossed, he looked down and saw his own shadow reflected in the water beneath. Thinking it was another dog with another piece of meat, he made up his mind to have that also. So he made a snap at the shadow in the water, but, as he opened his mouth, the piece of meat fell out,

dropped into the water and was never more seen. Beware, lest you lose the substance by grasping at the shadow.

Many people, like the dog in Aesop's fable, exchange the Truth of God for Satan's lies, and as a result, end up with nothing (see Romans 1:25).

Responsibility and Relationships

Satan desperately desires that by the time one realizes the hopelessness of associating with him, it will be too late. The hopelessness associated with the worldly relationship triad may not be immediately evident. That is because man does not have direct access to the hopelessness/death relationship. In other words, man does not come into direct contact with that relationship. (Refer back to figure 4-7.) Man must infer that relationship based on the two relationships in which he does have direct access. One usually discovers through the futility of walking by sight, over and over again, the vanity of it all. Likewise, man must infer the hope relationship of the spiritual triad based on the relationships in which he has direct access. Of course, Scripture reveals that the love of God, the Word of God, and the Spirit of God all testify to the hope we have. The arrangement of the spiritual and worldly triads also demonstrates man's responsibility when it comes to living by faith or by sight. Satan cannot make a person live by sight, and therefore sin, because Satan does not have direct access to that relationship. (Refer back to figure 4-7.) He can only motivate that person with self-love, enable him through deception, and empower him through the spirit of falsehood. In the same way, God does not control whether one walks by faith. He motivates with love, enables with the Word of Truth, and empowers through the work of the Holy Spirit. As Paul states, "Hope does not disappoint us, because God has poured out his love into our hearts by the Holy Spirit, whom he has given us" (Romans 5:5). This hope gradually becomes an additional motivating factor as we live by faith (see 1 Thessalonians 1:3). With regard to the manner in which God motivates us to live a life of faith: Love gives a shove and hope throws a rope.

An Illustration: The Testimony

You probably have heard someone give a personal testimony of how God changed his or her life. Indeed, you may have one of your own. Let us take a moment and think about the way a typical testimony is given in the context of our seven relationships and the defining and redefining of the soul. The speaker usually begins by painting a word picture of his previous life. This picture includes the relationship he had with the world and his life of sin. His life was all about him. No one else mattered. If it felt good, he did it. And the terrible things he did. He typically goes into some detail about his past sins. At some point, this deceptive life of self-gratification (self-love relationship) and sin (walking by sight relationship) showed its true nature, and the speaker inferred that there was no hope (death and hopelessness relationship) in the life he was living. Maybe he was arrested, maybe he overdosed, maybe he lost his family, or maybe he was tired of going in circles and he was ready to commit suicide. Whatever happened, it was the final straw, and he was near the end of his worldly journey. The despair of hopelessness had him in its grip. Finally, he heard for the first time about a real love, a love demonstrated to us (love relationship) by One who would give up His life for a man as decadent and evil as he had been. He listened to the Word of God, and the Holy Spirit convicted him of his sin. Immediately, he gave his life to Christ, submitted to His Lordship, and began to walk (faith relationship) with Him. Now, as he lives by faith, he knows that he truly has hope (hope relationship). Now that he has found something worth living for he wants to share his joy with others.

I am not trivializing or minimizing testimonials. Countless souls have begun the process of redefinition through testimonials. A testimonial not only substantiates the power of God's love, it also substantiates the relationships that define, and potentially redefine, the soul. The one giving the testimony is baring his soul, and every vowel and consonant he speaks fits within the parameters set forth in our model. First, he defines his soul by his relationship with Satan and the world and the things of this world. The discovery of the futility or hopelessness of these relationships led to despair. Through building new relationships with God and the things grounded in God, he found real hope. Paul writes, "Do not conform any longer to the pattern of this world, but be transformed by the renewing of your mind. Then you will be able to test and approve what God's will is—his good, pleasing and perfect will" (Romans 12:2). This transformation, or redefinition, is a "moving up" in the relationships that define your soul. This redefinition occurs when you stop defining your soul by relationships to things that are less than God and begin to define your soul through relationships with God. This moving up is diagrammed in the context of the spirit and soul. (See figure 4-8.)

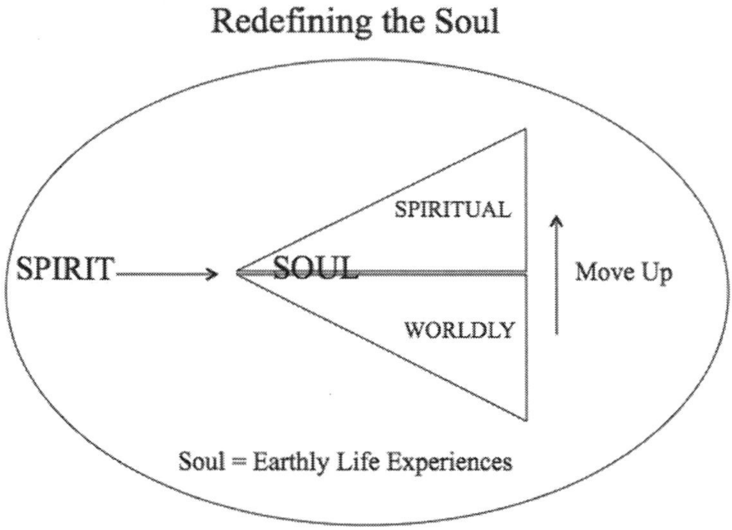

Redefining the Soul

SPIRIT → SOUL

SPIRITUAL

WORLDLY

↑ Move Up

Soul = Earthly Life Experiences

Figure 4-8

CHAPTER 5

REDEFINING THE SOUL – THE ALTERNATIVES

Some Personal Observations

Based on my academic and practical training in the field of psychology, I want to make several personal observations. First, I firmly believe that most personal problems people deal with—especially the kinds of problems that lead to hopelessness and despair—are a direct result of living apart from the will of God. Every theory of psychotherapy attributes pathological problems to a source that is congruent with its theoretical presuppositions. This source is often referred to as the "reason for pathology" and might include unconscious motivational conflict, dysfunctional interpersonal relationships, faulty learning, and faulty cognitions to name a few. We cannot immediately reject these causal factors, because some may indeed be implicated as a cause of problems that lead to despair, inasmuch as they constitute a deviation from the will of God. God is the Creator of all things, and living within the will of God means that we are functioning wholly, in both the earthly and spiritual realms, as God intended. Living within the will of God means we are living harmoniously with the pattern God has set, rather than against it.

A second observation is that the closer one lives to the will of God the less his or her life will be negatively affected by the kinds of problems that lead to hopelessness and despair. God's moral law is profitable to all in some measure and available to all in some measure. At the least, the moral law, congruent with the will of God, has been "written on man's heart" (Romans 2:15) and is visible in God's creation (see Romans 1:18-21). Additionally, thanks to the religious beliefs of the founding fathers of the United States of America, many societal laws and values still reflect some of God's truth and, therefore, provide guidance for life. Finally, whether most people in our culture claim to be believers or not, they have some knowledge of God and His commandments. Generally speaking, a person who lives a productive, peaceful life lives within the will of God or at least close to the will of God. In contrast, people whose lives are in shambles live far from the will of God in that their thoughts, words, and deeds are more often in direct opposition to Scriptural teaching.

A final observation is that living close to the will of God, rather than within the will of God, cannot fully satisfy (see Romans 14:23). One of Satan's deceptions is that close is good enough. The only true way to live within the will of God is by faith, and a saving faith must precede a living faith (see 2 Corinthians 5:7 and Colossians 2:12). As such, the single goal of "moving up," or redefining the soul, is to reconcile to God through a saving faith, and then to live within His will. Without a saving "faith it is impossible to please God" (Hebrews 11:6), and living by faith is synonymous to living within the will of God (see Hebrews 10:38).

I would guess, that in the last two decades, approximately twenty percent of the clients I have counseled would not consider themselves to be Christian. Some of these clients had a family member or friend who was a Christian that made the referral. Some intentionally sought out a Christian counselor and a smaller number were surprised, sometimes pleasantly, when they discovered I was a Christian counselor. Based on my belief that most personal problems people deal with—especially the kind of problems that lead to hopelessness and despair—are a direct result of living apart from the will of God, I feel an ethical responsibility to inform both Christian and non-Christian clients of my worldview. While it really should not surprise me, though it has on many occasions, I have not had a single client choose to go elsewhere because of this revelation. Why? Because people know in their hearts that there is a God and that there is a spiritual component to their personhood that is in serious need. This has been of great encouragement to me over the years and I share this experience to encourage others. Since Christians believe this premise to be true, that one cannot be truly fulfilled until they reconcile to God and live within His will, and it is true, we should be fully confident when we not only counsel the lost, but also when we evangelize the lost. They are searching and we have found what they are searching for.

By Faith

As Christians we are to "live by faith, not by sight" (2 Corinthians 5:7). Redefining the soul involves a "moving up" from the worldly triad to the spiritual triad. Redefining the soul implies a general focus on the soul or life of an individual as a collection of experiences and a specific focus on the faith relationship that forms that life. Faith is the life relationship through which we are to relate to new life experiences. Faith is also the life relationship through which we are to relate to past life experiences to bring them into a spiritual context. The current state of a human soul is defined by relationships and experiences from past to present. The possibilities of what that soul can become are found in the available relationships and experiences. Moving up is the result of building a faith relationship with God and His creation in a manner that pleases him.

Not only does Paul tell us that as Christians we are to live by faith, he also tells us "everything that does not come by faith is sin" (Romans 14:23). Paul is using the term faith here as a relationship that connects us to God's creation, all possible things that can be grounded in God. In this instance, Paul refers to faith not as saving faith, but as a reference to the confidence one has to make free use of what God has created. Likewise, the focus of this chapter is developing an appropriate faith relationship with God and His creation. Not because inappropriate relationships will necessarily lead to eternal condemnation, but because we desire to please God and live within His will.

The Source of Faith

Paul tells us that the Truth (Jesus Christ) communicated through the written Word of God is the source of faith (see Romans 10:17). Consequently, both a saving faith and a living faith must be fully grounded in God as He makes Himself known through His Word. Only when a person has faith in God can he or she have faith in His directives for life. When people live by faith, they do God's will regardless of the situation they face, and they continue to do God's will regardless of the consequences. They live on this earth; however, they are of God, and God is the source (motivating, enabling, and empowering) of their lives (by faith) (see 1 John 4:5, 6). The moral code by which a Christian lives is not grounded in the constantly changing philosophies and values of the world (see Colossians 2:8). The moral code a Christian lives by is grounded in an unchanging God (see Malachi 3:6 and Hebrews 13:8). The spiritual relationship triad is a constant. "There is one body and one Spirit—just as you were called to one hope when you were called—one Lord, one faith, one baptism; one God and Father of all, who is over all and through all and in all" (Ephesians 4:4-6). Additionally, God's expectations or directives are unchanging. "But the fruit of the Spirit is love, joy, peace, patience, kindness, goodness, faithfulness, gentleness and self-control. Against such things there is no law" (Galatians 5:22, 23). The Greek word translated fruit is not plural but singular. The fruit of the spirit is a single product with multiple qualities. The source of faith is a constant, just as the product of faith is a constant.

Additionally, the moral code by which a Christian lives is not based on outcome. It is grounded in God. Of course, we all have difficulties in this world; however, Christians striving to live within the will of God have the hope that they will find peace and be victorious in the end. When faced with difficult situations, we examine our thoughts, words, and deeds to ensure that they are in keeping with the will of God. We rectify what is lacking, and we find confidence, regardless of the outcome, living in His will. When we live by faith, we ground or establish our thoughts, words, and deeds in Christ Jesus, and Christ Jesus has "overcome the world" (John 16:33).

In contrast, a person living by sight, yet, close to the will of God cannot ground his or her life in God. The world deceives man with an ever-changing variety of lies. Some choose to believe there is no God and adopt a philosophy that a life of self-imposed morals is sufficient. Some find solace in that they believe in God and never are exposed to the necessity of loving Christ and keeping His commandments (see John 14:15). Many are drawn away and taken "captive through hollow and deceptive philosophy, which depends on human tradition and the basic principles of this world rather than on Christ" (Colossians 2:8). The world constantly changes to appeal to each individual's selfish desires like shifting shadows. "Just wait a minute," the world declares, "what you need is coming." Such people have lives grounded in their own conscience and the culture in which they live. As such, the direction of their lives is dependent on conscience, societal norms, and outcome.

It is true that many people who live in the worldly realm appear to lead lives similar to Christians. The difference is that their lives are founded in probability. They desire to have respectful children, faithful spouses, dependable friends, and to lead peaceful lives. They have reasoned or learned what lifestyle would most likely lead to lives they seek, and as long as the outcome is what they are looking for, they will likely make no changes. Their lifestyle is founded in probabilities. In the less-than-probable instance where the outcome is different from what they want, or when faced with eternal questions that a crisis such as illness, divorce or financial setback brings, they seek additional direction or change their lifestyles. Their lives are based on probability and outcome, nothing more and nothing less.

The Fruit of Faith

God has a love relationship with every person; however, only through an initial act of saving faith does a person reciprocate and fulfill that relationship. Once a person is in the correct relationship with God, a life of faith is expected. A life of faith is one wherein every earthly life experience, the substance of the human soul, is approached with an attitude of desire to please God. A life of faith is one that attempts to bring every thought, word, and deed into agreement with the will of God (see Colossians 3:17). God commands us to abstain from specific thoughts, words, and deeds. We are forbidden to covet, lie, or steal. The things from which we are commanded to abstain we can relate to only by sight. God also commands us to engage is specific thoughts, words, and deeds. For example, we are required to love one another, speak truthfully to one another, and give of our wealth to God. Many of God's commands can be related to either by faith or by sight. Those who ground their lives in the world can love, speak the truth, and give of their wealth the same as those who ground their lives in God; however, only when one does so by faith does he please God and live within His will. Once again, this brings us to an awareness of the importance of redefining our souls through a faith relationship. It is the faith relationship that connects our love relationship with God to His directives for our lives and, therefore, grounds or establishes our lives in God.

Is the issue, "Give me peace" or is it, "Make me a peace tree"? Faith is the process by which the new self produces thoughts, words, and deeds. The process dictates the product, and the product reflects on the process. It is faith and faith alone that leads to righteousness. If one wants to change the product, one must change the process by which it was formed. If a tree claims to be an apple tree yet has pears hanging on its branches, something is wrong. Likewise, if one claims to be a peace tree and produces discord, something is askew. Of course, such behavior is hypocrisy, and Jesus himself spoke strong words against such things. Jesus said, "Isaiah was right when he prophesied about you hypocrites; as it is written: 'These people honor me with their lips, but their hearts are far from me'" (Mark 7:6). And again, "Woe to you, teachers of the law and Pharisees, you hypocrites! You are like whitewashed tombs, which look beautiful on the outside but on the inside are full of dead men's bones and everything unclean" (Matthew 23:27). Christian purity signifies agreement within the process and between the process and the product. We must examine the process to appraise the quality of the product. A person may keep God's commandments; however, if it is not by faith, it cannot please God, because only by faith are His commandments grounded in Him.

Free Will—A Perpetual Fork in the Road

As long as we live as Christians, we stand at a perpetual fork in the road. (See figure 5-1.) Every moment of every day we are faced with a decision to live by faith or by sight. That is why we must understand the relationships involved in redefining the soul. Moving up to the spiritual triad allows us to live more fully within the will of God. We experience a harmony with our Creator as we interact with His creation according to His will. This results in a life of peace, joy, and contentment. Living within the will of God makes one effective in the work done for the Kingdom of God and will make one's "calling and election sure" (2 Peter 1:8-11). Living within the will of God ensures that one's thoughts, words, and deeds glorify God and work to His pleasure (see Romans 8:28).

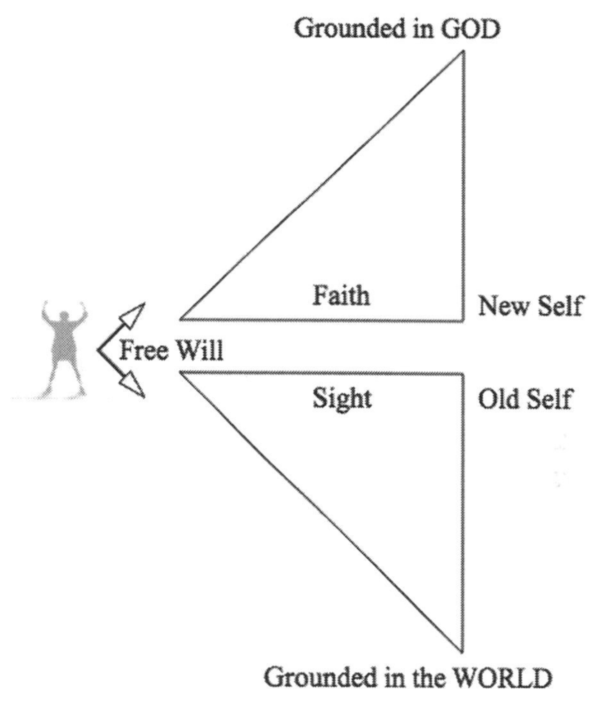

Figure 5-1

Why do Christians, saved by faith, sometimes choose to live by sight? First, we must accept that even as Christians we function in the earthly realm. As such, we will be tempted by the world's deceptions, and all will sin. Too often, people compartmentalize their lives whereby they live by faith as best they can in one area, yet, allow the world to guide their decisions and live by sight in another. For example, a person may live according to God's will in his personal life and play by the world's rules in his professional life. Often it is simply a matter of maturity. Many people deviate from the will of God out of ignorance; they simply do not know what the will of God is. If a life of faith must be grounded in God, one must know God to live a life of faith. We please God by faith, living according to His will, and His will is made known to us through His Word. One ignorant of His Word will find it difficult to live by faith. To the degree we live by faith, to that degree our thoughts, words, and deeds will glorify God. To the degree we live by faith, to that degree we will experience peace. To the degree we live by faith, to that degree we will be effective in the work we do in his Kingdom.

Living by Sight

Scripture teaches that we should set our hearts and minds on things that are above, things that are pure and praiseworthy (see Colossians 3:1 and Philippians 4:8). However, Scripture also provides some basic information regarding free will, temptation and sin. Satan's desire is that man live apart from the will of God, because that which is apart from the will of God is lawlessness, and "sin is lawlessness" (1 John 3:4). God allowed the possibility of sin into the world when He "commanded the man, 'You are free to eat from any tree in the garden; but you must not eat from the tree of the knowledge of good and evil, for when you eat of it you will surely die'" (Genesis 2:16, 17). Through this commandment to abstain from eating from the tree of the knowledge of good and evil, Adam and Eve were given a choice, and through that choice they became free agents. It was not probable that they—even as free agents—would exercise their will against God, because Adam and Eve knew nothing of evil. Their hearts and minds were pure and in complete harmony with the will of God. It was Satan, manifesting himself in the form of a serpent, who took the possibility of sin and increased it to a probability with the introduction of a lie: "'You will not surely die,' the serpent said to the woman" (Genesis 3:4). Through Satan's lie, evil was introduced into the heart and mind of man. When the evil of Satan's lies united with man's natural desires (food, things pleasing to the eye, and wisdom), desires previously met in ways that pleased God, temptation was born. When man acted in accordance with that temptation and apart from the will of God, sin entered into the world (see Romans 5:12). While Satan is the source of evil, man has become corrupted by sin and is a "carrier" of evil (see Romans 3:23; 5:12).

James affirms that temptation occurs when the deception of evil and man's desires come together. James writes, "When tempted, no one should say, "God is tempting me." For God cannot be tempted by evil, nor does He tempt anyone; but each one is tempted when, by his own evil desire, he is dragged away and enticed. Then, after desire has conceived, it gives birth to sin; and sin, when it is full-grown, gives birth to death" (James 1:13-15). Desire is a motivational energy that wells up from within man and may be founded in a God-given need, as in the need for food or purpose, or an acquired need of corrupted man, as in the need for drugs or power. The deceptive evil that unites to that desire can be from within man, who has been corrupted, or can be introduced from the outside, the world. James emphasizes that temptation is not synonymous with sin. Temptation is simply the specific understanding of how we can attempt to feed a desire in a way that is against God. When temptation drags man away from God and entices man to act in a way that is against God, sin is born (see James 1:15). Conception occurs when man chooses to act on the deceptive evil and thereby substitutes his will for the will of God. When man is tempted, and then chooses or wills to extend the temptation into continued thought or action, the temptation becomes sin.

Satan and the world conspire to motivate man to walk by sight by deceiving man into believing he can satisfy his needs in a way that is apart from God. Satan motivates man to sin through man's own love of self, and Satan's schemes are founded in deception and testified to by the spirit of falsehood. If we are able to discern the lies, we are able to infer the hopelessness.

Three "Ways" of Temptation

Hebrews 14:15 declares that Jesus was "tempted in every way, just as we are—yet was without sin." Of course, Jesus did not experience every individual temptation you or I or any other person has or will experience; yet, Jesus was tempted in the same general ways. We know that temptation occurs when evil, originating within an individual or introduced from an outside source, creates an awareness of a manner in which needs can be met apart from the will of God. In Jesus' case the evil was from without, because Jesus was sinless, and He had no evil within (see 2 Corinthians 5:21). It was evil in the world, specifically introduced by Satan himself, which made contact with Jesus' needs and desires. Satan desires that we live or function in the worldly relationship triad; motivated by self-love, living by sight, and inferring something of value from it all but ending in hopelessness. The three ways in which we are tempted relate to the world, rather than to God, and are specified in 1 John 2:16 and include the lust of the flesh, the lust of the eyes, and the pride of life. Each temptation has a corresponding relationship in the worldly triad. The lust of the flesh corresponds to the man-world relationship (self-love); it is motivated by love of self and consists of temptations that we believe will meet our physical and sensual needs. The lust of the eyes corresponds to the man-things of the world relationship (sight); it is motivated by the desire to live by sight, and consists of things aesthetic and pleasing to the eye. The pride of life corresponds to the world - old-self relationship (death/hopelessness); it is inferred as a hope relationship, while in reality it is vain and meaningless and holds no hope. (See figure 5-2.)

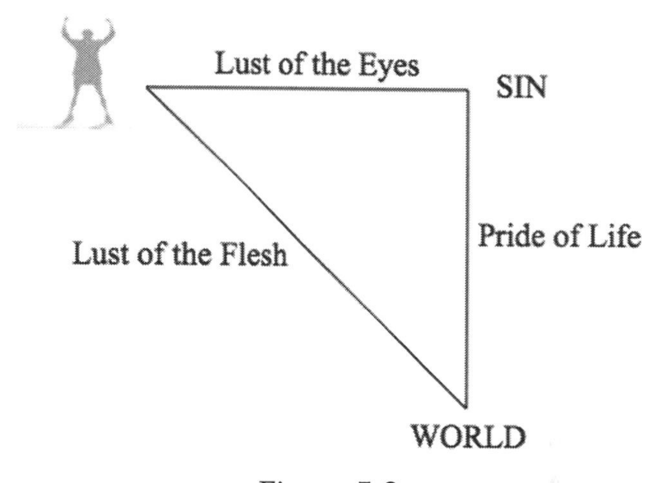

Figure 5-2

Scripture records three temptations of Jesus, each corresponding to one of the three ways every man is tempted. Satan attempted to have Jesus satisfy His needs and desires apart from God through the three relationships in the worldly triad. Read that passage carefully here:

> [1]Then Jesus was led by the Spirit into the desert to be tempted by the devil. [2]After fasting forty days and forty nights, he was hungry. [3]The tempter came to him and said, "If you are the Son of God, tell these stones to become bread." [4]Jesus answered, "It is written: 'Man does not live on bread alone, but on every word that comes from the mouth of God.'" [5]Then the devil took him to the holy city and had him stand on the highest point of the temple. [6]"If you are the Son of God," he said, "throw yourself down. For it is written: "'He will command his angels concerning you, and they will lift you up in their hands, so that you will not strike your foot against a stone.'" [7]Jesus answered him, "It is also written: 'Do not put the Lord your God

> to the test.'" [8]Again, the devil took him to a very high mountain and showed him all the kingdoms of the world and their splendor. [9]"All this I will give you," he said, "if you will bow down and worship me." [10]Jesus said to him, "Away from me, Satan! For it is written: 'Worship the Lord your God, and serve him only.'" [11]Then the devil left him, and angels came and attended him. (Matthew 4:1-11)

Jesus' first temptation, recorded in verse 3, focused on man's need for food and nourishment (lust of the flesh). Jesus' second temptation, recorded in verse 6, focused on man's desire for significance (pride of life). Jesus' third temptation, recorded in verse 9, focused on man's desire for things that are pleasing to the eye (lust of the eyes). When Eve was tempted in the Garden of Eden to eat of the tree of the knowledge of good and evil, that single temptation was related by Eve to all three worldly relationships. Eve saw that the fruit was pleasing to look at (lust of the eyes), would be good for physical nourishment (lust of the flesh) and desirable for gaining wisdom and significance (pride of life) (see Genesis 3:6).

So, what exactly does the world have to offer man? That question has already been tested by such a one as Solomon, and the results are recorded in the book of Ecclesiastes. Kidwell (1977) notes that living in the worldly relationship triad "results in meaninglessness, nothing more—and there is nothing less. As we attempt to meet our needs apart from God, we discover that no new road can be traveled that man has not already traveled. Though it appears that man is discovering new ways to find happiness, he is merely inventing new names to define and describe ancient pursuits. And the paradox remains that those with the most wealth and resources to invest in meeting their needs and desires in ways apart from God have the greatest need" (p. xvi).

The Depressive Triad

As illustrated in the testimony from the last chapter, functioning in the worldly triad leads us to discover that no lasting satisfaction can be found when we meet our needs through the world and the things of the world. When man discovers the world has nothing to offer and that the end result of functioning in the worldly triad is meaningless, the response is often depression, despair, and hopelessness. The Depressive Triad is often discussed as a diagnostic tool for depression in both secular and Christian texts (see Beck, 1979, as an example). The depressive triad forms in a person's life when he or she comes to the realization that the world cannot satisfy their needs. The resulting experience is a negative view of self, a negative view of the world, and a negative view of the future. (See figure 5-3.) When a person feels worthless and insignificant and realizes that he or she lives in a world with nothing of value to offer, the future becomes bleak. The result is often depression, despair, and suicidal behavior.

Depressive Triad

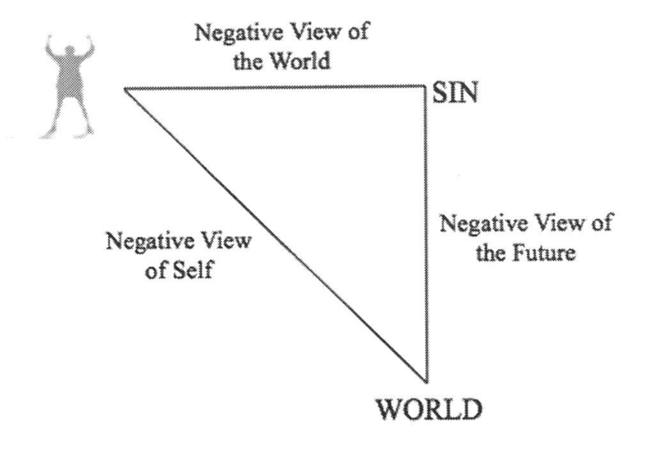

Figure 5-3

Christians can experience the depressive triad when they insist on deviating from the will of God and rely instead on what the world offers. Living fully in the spiritual triad makes one immune to the effects of the depressive triad. A Christian, who is thinking as God would have them think, will not have a negative view of self. What can make one more significant than the fact that the God of all creation sent His one and only Son to die for him (see John 3:16) and adopts him as a joint heir to that Son (see Ephesians 1:5 and Galatians 4:7)? Living in the world can be difficult; however, we know that "to live is Christ" (Philippians 1:21). And what of the future? Well, the hope of the future "does not disappoint us because God has poured out His love into our hearts by the Holy Spirit, whom he has given us" (Romans 5:5). Man is free to choose his path, however, as the author of Ecclesiastes concluded; in the end, the only wise choice is that we revere and worship the One True God and live harmoniously within His will (see Ecclesiastes 12:13).

CHAPTER 6

REDEFINING THE SOUL – BY FAITH

A Saving Faith to a Living Faith

Living by sight, outside the will of God, leads to despair. We know that as Christians we are to live by faith and that anything that does not both originate and proceed from faith is a sin. We also know that it is through a faith relationship that the soul is redefined. Our interest now shifts to this most important question; "What does it mean to live by faith?" We begin by examining faith as a saving relationship that reconciles one to God. We will then examine faith as a life relationship that facilitates Christian maturity and a life that grows within the will of God. Faith, as a condition for salvation, is a synthesis of two components. First, one must believe the Word of God. The Word of God is Jesus (see John 1:14), so this belief is specifically that Jesus is the Christ, the Son of the living God and salvation comes through Him (see Romans 10:9).

Belief is a judgment made at a cognitive level. The second component of the synthesis of a saving faith is trust. Trust is shown in the way our belief is manifested in our lives and expressed through our behaviors. One believes by coming to a conclusion that something is true, and then one trusts in that conclusion. One believes that salvation comes through Jesus Christ, and then trusts Jesus Christ to secure his hope. One believes by hearing the Word of God and consequently repents of sin, confesses Christ as Lord, and is baptized into the Body of Christ. This synthesis of belief and trust is the means by which one is saved. It is a saving faith. It is a faith that reconciles us to our Creator.

When we begin to examine faith as a life relationship that leads to Christian maturity, we discover that we are expected to develop our faith. A saving faith brings one into the correct relationship with God, and living faith then develops, allowing one to mature in that relationship. The components of a saving faith (belief and trust) expand and grow into a living faith. James declares that a living faith manifests itself in action, a natural extension of trust. James tells us, "faith without works is dead" (James 2:17). If one chooses to believe something is true, he places his trust in that truth and consequently will act in accordance with that belief. Paul states, "for it is God who works in you to will (belief) and to act (trust) according to his good purpose" (Philippians 2:13). Paul later becomes very specific and writes, "Finally, brothers, whatever is true, whatever is noble, whatever is right, whatever is pure, whatever is lovely, whatever is admirable—if anything is excellent or praiseworthy—think about such things" (Philippians 4:8). Paul then continues with, "Whatever you have learned or received or heard from me, or seen in me—put it into practice" (Philippians 4:9). So, a living faith includes believing and trusting, willing and acting, or thinking and putting into practice. (See figure 6-1.)

	Saving Faith	
Belief		**Trust**
	Living Faith	
Faith		**Works**
Will		**Act**
Think		**Put into Practice**

Figure 6-1

Is a living faith something different than a saving faith? A living faith is simply a more mature, fuller expression of a saving faith. An embryo has life, and that life continues as the individual matures into an adult. Are an embryo and adult the same? Yes, but the adult is a mature and fuller expression of the embryo. A saving faith brings new birth to man, and a living faith continues to develop that original saving faith into a mature Christian faith. Paul referred to this maturation process when he told the church at Galatia "I am again in the pains of childbirth until Christ is formed in you" (Galatians 4:19).

A more detailed delineation of a faith relationship is found in 2 Peter 1:5-11. This passage refers to both a saving faith and a living faith, as Peter refers to the process as necessary for salvation, verses 10, 11, and for Christian maturity, verse 8.

> [5]"For this very reason, make every effort to add to your faith goodness; and to goodness, knowledge; [6]and to knowledge, self-control; and to self-control, perseverance; and to perseverance, godliness; [7]and to godliness, brotherly kindness; and to brotherly kindness, love. [8]For if you possess these qualities in increasing measure, they will keep you from being ineffective

and unproductive in your knowledge of our Lord Jesus Christ. [9]But if anyone does not have them, he is nearsighted and blind, and has forgotten that he has been cleansed from his past sins. [10]Therefore, my brothers, be all the more eager to make your calling and election sure. For if you do these things, you will never fall, [11]and you will receive a rich welcome into the eternal kingdom of our Lord and Savior Jesus Christ."

Peter tells us that to be effective and productive as Christians, and to make our calling and election sure, we should add to or develop our faith. We add to or develop our faith with the qualities of goodness, knowledge, self-control, and perseverance. When this list of qualities is examined in the context of both a saving and living faith, we discover they expand on and harmonize with the two components of faith (belief-trust, faith-works, will-act and think-practice) previously examined. (See figure 6-2.)

Saving Faith

Belief	Trust

Living Faith

Faith	Works
Will	Act
Think	Put into Practice
Goodness/Knowledge	Self-Control/Perseverance

Figure 6-2

As we develop our faith, we begin with goodness (sometimes translated virtue). Goodness or virtue is an attitude of readiness or a predisposition to please God. Goodness is an attitude of the heart, the beginning point for our thoughts, words and deeds. If the heart is corrupt, the whole of man is corrupt. Goodness indicates that one is prepared to act in some way consistent with saving faith. Second, we are to add knowledge. Knowledge must be stored in the soul to be useful. We have a predisposition to please God; now we must know what, specifically, it is that pleases God. This knowledge is of the will of God and therefore must come from the Word of God. Third, we add self-control. We have a predisposition to please God. We know from the Word what God's will is. Now we reason based on the situation at hand and the spiritual knowledge in the soul so that we might act in a way that is pleasing to God and a blessing to his Kingdom. Self-control, or reasoning, is a function of the mind. Finally, we add perseverance. We will not always be successful as we attempt to live as God wants us to. When we fail, we acknowledge the failure and try again. We must find the strength to continue to run the race. If the outcome is confusing in that we are unsure, we reflect to confirm that our thoughts, words and deeds were grounded in God, and we persevere.

While there are many narratives in Scripture that support this delineation of the faith relationship, we'll focus our thoughts on two final examples. The first example harmonizes effortlessly with the passage from 2 Peter. How did Jesus respond when asked about the greatest commandment (see Mark 12:28)? Jesus responded, "Love the Lord your God with all your heart (goodness) and with all your soul (knowledge) and with all your mind (self-control) and with all your strength (perseverance)" (Mark 12:30). Jesus follows this command with a second command to "love your neighbor as yourself" (see Mark 12:31). Loving one's neighbor is the product of a living faith, as is, "godliness, brotherly kindness and love" from the Second Peter passage (see 2 Peter 1:7). (See figure 6-3.)

Saving Faith	
Belief	Trust
Living Faith	
Faith	Works
Will	Act
Think	Put into Practice
Goodness / Knowledge	Self-Control / Perseverance
Heart / Soul	Mind / Strength

Figure 6-3

The final example requires some thought to harmonize with what has been established thus far. James also addresses the development of a living faith. He writes; "Consider it pure joy, my brothers, whenever you face trials of many kinds, because you know that the testing of your faith develops perseverance. Perseverance must finish its work so that you may be mature and complete, not lacking anything" (James 1:2-4). An initial comparison would lead one to think that the passage from James is inconsistent with the passage from Second Peter. James states, "The testing of your faith develops perseverance." The Second Peter passage inserts goodness, knowledge and self-control between faith and perseverance. A closer inspection of the James passage, however, resolves what appears to be an inconsistency. James continues with, "If any of you lacks wisdom, he should ask God, who gives generously to all without finding fault, and it will be given to him" (James 1:5). Wisdom as a human attribute is the ability to take information (knowledge) and apply it (self-control) in an effective and efficient manner. Recall that Brown (1986) stated, "the concept of mind comes nearest to the concept of wisdom" (v. 2, p. 620). Wisdom is both knowledge and the ability to put that knowledge into practice. We now see that the James passage aligns or harmonizes more fully with the Second Peter passage. Of course, if we include knowledge and self-control (wisdom) to perseverance, we are still missing the quality of goodness, which is a predisposition to please God, in the James passage, the goodness that is present in Second Peter. James resolves this difference later where he speaks of two kinds of wisdom: wisdom from below and wisdom from above (see James 3:15-17). The world's wisdom is not synonymous with the wisdom from God. Wisdom from God begins with an attitude of readiness to please God, that is, goodness. So, if we paraphrase the James passage, we may have something like, "The testing of our faith develops perseverance, and if anyone lacks goodness, knowledge, and self-control, that is, the wisdom from above, he should ask God." While there are many Bible narratives that would continue to offer support of this process of a living faith, we will be satisfied with adding the words of Jesus and the writings of James. (See figure 6-4.)

Saving Faith

Belief	Trust

Living Faith

Faith	Works
Will	Act
Think	Put into Practice
Goodness / Knowledge	Self-Control / Perseverance
Heart / Soul	Mind / Strength
Wisdom from Above (Goodness, Knowledge, Self-Control)	Perseverance

Figure 6-4

Christian Purity

A number of years ago, a colleague came into my office and asked what my thoughts were concerning a specific topic in an academic field of study. I began my response to the inquiry with something like, "Well the Bible actually addresses that in some . . ." at which point my colleague's hands flew up in the air as if to say "stop" followed by a reply of, "Oh my, I don't want to Christianize this discussion." We then conversed briefly and superficially about the topic at hand and my colleague left my office. I recall being a bit perplexed after that incident. Was I incorrect for Christianizing the matter and did I fail to effectively meet the needs of my colleague?

As stated earlier in this chapter, Christian purity signifies agreement within the process of a living faith and between the process of that faith and the product of that faith (see 1 Timothy 1:4, 5). Purity within the process means that goodness, knowledge, self-control and perseverance are in agreement with each other. Each subsequent stage in the process is the natural extension of, and compliments, the previous stage. It is only when one begins with the proper attitude (goodness of the heart) that is predisposed to pleasing God, that one will seek and bring information into the soul (biblical knowledge) that is in accordance with His will. One's mind then becomes active as it analyzes (mindful self-control, spirit-soul relation) the information relevant to the situation at hand in the context of proper Christian conduct. One then is steadfast (strength to persevere) as one acts in a manner that compliments the character of one's heart, soul and mind and glorifies God. Any faltering at any stage in the development of the faith relationship would corrupt the relationship. This is why a corrupt heart, the beginning point of faith, corrupts the whole man.

Purity also signifies agreement between one's living faith and the product of that faith. A life of faith produces the fruit of the Spirit and the first expression of the fruit of the Spirit is love (see Galatians 5:22, 23). We also recall that Paul wrote, "the only thing that counts is faith expressing itself through love" (Ephesians 5:6b). Faith must be activated by love and expressed in love. Love serves a dual purpose as both the motivator of our faith and the final expression of that faith. In the second chapter of Revelation, Jesus addresses the church at Ephesus. He has some encouraging words for them as he states, "I know your deeds, your hard work and your perseverance. I know that you cannot tolerate wicked men, that you have tested those who claim to be apostles but are not, and have found them false. You have persevered and have endured hardships for my name, and have not grown weary" (Revelation 2:2, 3). Jesus immediately follows this with a stern admonition. He continues, "Yet I hold this against you: You have forsaken your first love. Remember the height from which you have fallen! Repent and do the things you did at first. If you do not repent, I will come to you and remove your lampstand from its place" (Revelation 2:4, 5). While the church at Ephesus was doing good things, corruption had infiltrated the process at some point and Jesus admonished them to return to the way they had been. Specifically, Jesus said they had "lost their first love." The word pairing first love literally means a love that is the primary placeholder and motivates one toward action. It's interesting that this word pairing only appears in this single verse where Jesus addresses the church at Ephesus. A little research into the history of Ephesus sheds some light on the meaning that this word pairing may have had for the Ephesians. The Ephesians had experienced their most prosperous and peaceful period under the rule of Alexander the Great. The teachings of Aristotle, who was Alexander's tutor, were well known and eagerly discussed throughout Ephesus. They now were following a new teaching, that of Jesus Christ, but the influence of Aristotle was still very much a part of their culture. One of Aristotle's well-known hypotheses was the necessity for all one's actions to spring forth from a proper first cause. The search for this first cause occupied much of Aristotle's thoughts and therefore, his discourses. Today we refer to this notion of a first cause as an "unmoved mover" in that it is the primary placeholder that motivates one toward action. According to Aristotle only actions that spring from a single and proper first cause, or unmoved mover, will lead to true happiness. The similarities are compelling between the words of Jesus and those of Aristotle. It was also common for Jesus to communicate using words and examples the hearer could identify with and easily understand. So what would this first love be? I think for most Christians it is obvious that our first love is the love we have for God and He for us. It is this love that should always be the unmoved mover of our life of faith. It is the love for others that should always be the product of that life of faith. How did Jesus reply when asked about the greatest commandment? He replied, "Love the Lord your God with all your heart and with all your soul and with all your mind and with all your strength.' The second is this: 'Love your neighbor as yourself.' There is no commandment greater than these" (Mark 12:30,31). A pure faith is motivated by love and expresses itself in love. A pure faith requires that we Christianize everything.

In All Things Pray

James reminds us of the importance of prayer as we live by faith. He also reminds us of the surety that God will help us to live a life pleasing to Him as he tells us that

God gives wisdom freely to all who ask with faith. The First Epistle of John supports this. John writes; "This is the confidence we have in approaching God: that if we ask anything according to his will, he hears us. And if we know that he hears us—whatever we ask—we know that we have what we asked of him" (1 John 5:14, 15). As children of God, we can be confident when we ask God for things within His will. We also know that it is within the will of God that we have the necessities to live by faith. So goodness, knowledge, self-control (wisdom), and perseverance are qualities God wants us to have. Therefore, we can be confident we will receive when we ask. How many of us really ask for what God wants us to have and what we really need to be spiritually mature? Do we pray for God to motivate, enable and empower us to bear the fruit of love, joy, peace, patience, kindness, goodness, faithfulness, gentleness and self-control? Or, do we continue to ask for health, financial security and a better job?

God has equipped us with everything necessary to live a life of faith, pleasing to Him. God motivates us through perfect love, enables us through His Word, and empowers us through the work of the Holy Spirit—all so that we can live lives of faith. We are responsible to adopt an attitude that desires to please God in all we do. We add to that attitude of desire to please God knowledge from his Word. We put that knowledge into practice and persevere under difficult circumstances.

Reason

The Apostle Paul speaks to the very thing we have been discussing. Christians are to forsake their worldly ways and replace them with a lifestyle pleasing to God. In Ephesians 4:22-25 Paul writes:

> You were taught, with regard to your former way of life, to put off your old self, which is being corrupted by its deceitful desires; to be made new in the attitude of your minds; and to put on the new self, created to be like God in true righteousness and holiness. Therefore each of you must put off falsehood and speak truthfully to his neighbor, for we are all members of one body.

As stated earlier, man can function in one of two ways. First, we can put things on autopilot and live both in the moment and for the moment. This manner of living is impulsive or instinctive (see Jude 10) and Scripture likens such a life to the "brute beasts of the fields" (2 Peter 2:12). A second and proper option for Christians is to reason. Christian reasoning takes place when the spirit and soul relate to choose the manner in which to respond in a specific situation. Now, it is true that one can reason to do evil (see Romans 1:30 and Genesis 6:5); however, God desires that we reason in a way that is consistent with a life of faith. That is why Scripture instructs us to "take every thought captive and make it submissive to the will of God" (2 Corinthians 10:5). In doing this, we consider the development of our faith and remain diligent to ensure that at all times we have an attitude of the heart that desires to please God (goodness, virtue). We use our minds to reason as we consider the circumstances and search God's Word for guidance (knowledge). We reason as we translate God's Word into our lives and allow it to be manifested in our thoughts, words, and deeds (self-control). And finally, when we fail or fall short of God's will, we reason and find strength in God to continue with what often seems the impossible (perseverance). As our faith develops, through the process of Christian reasoning, we discover that we are able to live more often within the will of God and that we indeed, begin to live more and more by faith.

CHAPTER 7

REDEFINING THE SOUL – TEMPTATIONS

Now, I am sure that all the foregoing makes sense to most believers. We know we should be doing all these things, and many will probably feel more of a sense of guidance on how to live more effectively within the will of God; they understand to a greater degree how to accomplish that goal. The problem comes in those difficult times where it seems almost impossible to overcome Satan, the evil one. How does one deal with temptations that are so powerful that resisting seems futile? And if one does manage to resist, won't the temptation just rear its ugly head again and again? Well, the answer is once again in Scripture, and it is very enlightening.

Fighting Temptation - The Seventh Relationship

Each time I read or think about the passage from James where he affirms that if you "resist the devil, he will flee from you" (James 4:7b), I am reminded of a specific temptation that I experienced in the summer of my eighteenth year. I actually knew then, as I was experiencing the temptation, that it was stronger than any sinful desire I had experienced to that point in my life. The specific temptation occurred on the final day of a very-long backpacking hike through the Rocky Mountains. We had been eating freeze-dried food for the week or so that we had been in the mountains and freeze-drying food was a fairly new technology in the 1970's. While the picture of the food on the package was appealing to the eye, all the food tasted the same and reminded me of what wallpaper paste might taste like. I hadn't really gone without many meals in the first eighteen years of my life, as my mother was an eager and excellent cook. By the time we began to work our way down out of the mountains all of us were looking forward to some real food – some of us more than others. We came to a staging area where day hikers had gathered and there on a fallen log sat a middle-aged man eating a round of Colby cheese. The moment I saw that cheese I wanted that cheese. Okay now reader, some of you are probably chuckling to yourself and wondering how food could be the source of such a temptation. If so, I'd refer you to the temptations of Eve, Esau and the first recorded temptation of Jesus. Now I'll get back to my story. While I knew that stealing was wrong, every undernourished cell in my body was screaming, "Feed me!" I began to rationalize and soon I had convinced myself that under these unusual circumstances it would be acceptable to steal that man's cheese. I used my mind to reason (wisdom from below) through all possible scenarios by which I might procure the cheese. I remember thinking I could just go up and explain my hunger and ask for the whole round of Colby, but then I realized he would probably think I was a nut, move to a safer location and take the cheese with him. He'd then keep an eye on "the nut" and protect his cheese so I'd not be able to easily implement any plan I might devise. I then came back to the only option; I'd run by him, snatch the cheese and disappear in the woods where I could feast on it. My spirit really did desire to do God's will and I knew that stealing that cheese was absolutely the wrong thing to do but I just didn't know how to resist the devil. My spirit was willing, but my flesh was weak (see Matthew 26:41).

You might say I have been a student of temptation most of my life and as a result I have discovered a few important things along the way. The most important thing I've discovered is that Scripture provides the means by which we can be triumphant over temptation - and actually make the devil flee. The seventh relationship possesses some necessary qualities that facilitate our fight against temptation and sin. Remember that the seventh relationship is the relationship between the spiritual and worldly triads. As noted earlier, the seventh relationship is always negative in that the two triads, spiritual and worldly, are dissonant to each other. In other words, there is total and complete disagreement between everything in the spiritual triad and everything in the worldly triad. This negative or dissonant relationship is a key element in the fight against temptation and sin. (See figure 7-1.)

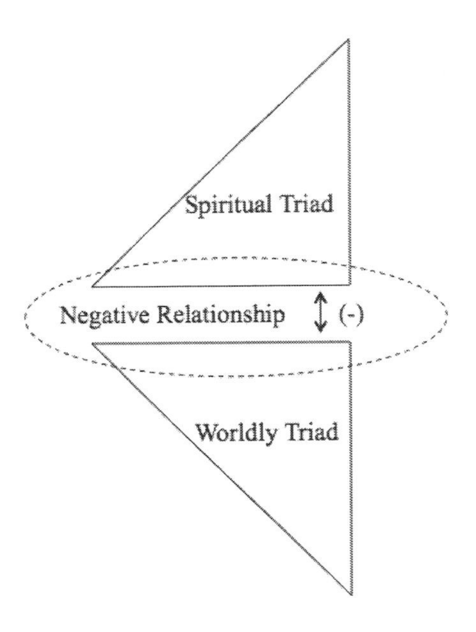

Figure 7-1

In this exploration into the seventh relationship, various laws of science will be mentioned. While these laws of science augment our understanding, what is most important is what Scripture says about this relationship. The first feature of the seventh relationship, relevant to the process of dealing with temptation, is a specific aspect of what science refers to as the "law of opposites." For our purposes, this will be conceptualized as the truth that opposites cannot coexist. Scripture tells us that "freshwater and saltwater cannot flow from the same spring" (James 3:11) and that light cannot fellowship with darkness (see 1 John 2:9). While Paul instructs us to put off the old self and put on the new self, there are times we find it difficult to put off the old self. God promises that He will not allow us to be tempted beyond what we can endure (see 1 Corinthians 10:13); however, sometimes it feels as though a temptation is too strong to overcome. When one is dealing with temptations, it is good to reverse Paul's statement and put on the new self to put off the old self. Actually, examples from Scripture support the idea that we put off the old self by putting on the new self. Let me share an analogy with you. In 1978 I was enrolled in a 7:00 a.m. Johannine Epistles course with Professor Sherwood Smith. The students were mostly freshman and sophomores, and a glance around the room on any given morning provided evidence of why 7:00 a.m. classes were destined to end. While I will admit to being only half awake during most of the lectures, I probably learned as much in that course as in any course I have taken. I remember Professor Smith saying something like this:

> Listen up, class. I want you to really hear this. John tells us that light cannot fellowship with darkness, but I want you to really appreciate the power of light. Let me tell you a story that happened to me recently. We were visiting Mammoth Cave in Kentucky, and the tour guide was taking us deep into the cave. We came to a very large room in the cave, and the tour guide explained that we were far enough into the cave that there was no longer any light from the entrance and that without the electrical lights it would be completely black. She said that total darkness in a cave was different than darkness in the world above and that she wanted us to experience it so she was going to turn off all the electric lights. We were instructed to turn off any lights that might be on our camera flashes, and then she started at "ten" and began a countdown to lights off. When she reached "one," she turned a lever and the lights went out. As we stood there in a complete darkness few of us had experienced before, she proceeded to explain how darkness was really nothing other than the absence of light. She said we often speak of "darkness falling" or "darkness coming on,"

> but it is really that light is leaving. Suddenly, we saw a spark then the pulsing flame from a single wooden match that our tour guide had lit. It was nowhere near the brightness of the electric lights; however, our tour guide noted that even the light from a single match was able to illuminate the distant walls of such a large room. I thought to myself that's the way God's Word functions in a dark world. The world is living in darkness and thinks that darkness is something, but it is really only an absence of light. Christians are the light of the world, the bearers of the Good News, and their job is to dispel the darkness around them. Listen up class, it is a truthful statement that to whatever degree light is introduced, darkness is dispelled.

I pondered that statement for many years. "To whatever degree light is introduced, darkness is dispelled." As my interest in psychology developed, my understanding of that statement broadened. I no longer exclusively applied the principle to the darkness in the world; I began to apply the concept to darkness in the human soul. Just as darkness is nothing but the absence of light, the human soul is meaningless without God. Additionally, to put off darkness all one needs to do is put on light. To put off evil, all one needs to do is put on righteousness. To put off anxiety, put on the peace that passes all understanding (see Philippians 4). To put off fear, put on love (see 1 John 4:8). To put off deceit, put on truthfulness (see Ephesians 4:25). Is your soul full of darkness? Get rid of the darkness by putting on light, for what fellowship can light have with darkness? It's a powerful concept, and its power lies in the seventh relationship, the relationship between the spiritual and worldly relationship triads: always negative. If two things cannot coexist, to the degree you put on one, to that degree you put off the other.

James affirms that if you "resist the devil, he will flee from you" (James 4:7b). The manner in which one resists lies in James's words directly before and after this passage. James begins by saying, "Submit yourselves, then, to God" (James 4:7a). He then follows that with the instruction to resist the devil, and then he continues with, "Come near to God and he will come near to you" (verse 8a). So to resist the devil (darkness) you submit yourselves to God and come near to God (light). To whatever degree light is introduced, darkness is dispelled. The Greek word translated resist could also be translated oppose. I prefer that, because resist conveys an idea of standing firm against something, while oppose is more actively moving away from something. To oppose Satan, we actively move away from him toward God. To oppose darkness, we actively move away from it toward light.

This idea of two dissonant things being unable to coexist becomes even more relevant in the context of a quality that all humans possess. God created man able to think about, or attend to, only one thing at a time. Psychologists call this serial processing, and it is a limitation of all humans. You might have to reflect a bit to accept this; however, you are like everyone else, and you can attend to only one thing at a time. A common example of this occurs when you read something, like this book, while you are actually attending to, or thinking about, something else. At some point, you stop and realize that you have not comprehended anything you have read. It is the limitation of serial processing that facilitates the existence of Attention-Deficit Hyperactivity Disorder (ADHD). A person with ADHD finds it difficult to focus his attention where it should be focused and finds that even a weak stimulus will divert his attention elsewhere. While all humans are limited by serial processing, there are a number of additional abilities that humans possess that allow them to function effectively given this limitation. For example, as already mentioned, people possess the ability to engage in subconscious or automatic behaviors such as reading and driving an automobile while attending to something else. Many of you have pulled into your driveway and realized that you were so caught up in thought that you do not even recall the drive home. Additionally, humans have the ability to switch attention very quickly between multiple stimuli when necessary. When one mentally solves a simple mathematics problem, attention jumps from number to number to mathematical rule very quickly. Finally, people have a form of memory that can "replay" the past fifteen seconds or so of information when they realize that they should have been attending to something. This instant replay ability is called short-term memory and it allows you to rewind, and therefore attend to, a limited amount of the material. This happens often in communication when we are attending to something other than what is being said and then a question is asked of us. We respond first with "What?" because we were not attending to the person speaking, and then we quickly replay the words from short-term memory and then follow up with a reply like, "Oh, that would be fine" as we answer the question.

One has to question why God would create man with such a limiting characteristic as that of serial processing. Two of the reasons that God created man to process serially have to do with control and responsibility. Because man can only attend to a single thing at any given time, man has control over that to which he will attend. In other words, man can choose to think about something and man can choose to think about something else. It is our choice if we set our minds on things that are true and noble (see Philippians 4:8). It is also our choice if we acknowledge sinful thoughts and replace them with thoughts that are righteous (see 2 Corinthians 10:5). The limitations of serial processing provide us with choices; however, it also clearly defines us as responsible for our choices.

We were created by God in such a way that it is impossible to attend to darkness if we choose to attend to light. Scripture tells us that we are to "take captive every thought and make it submissive to the will of God" (2 Corinthians 10:5). We get into trouble when we are tempted and we don't take the thought captive and make it submissive to God's will. In other words, we continue to contemplate, or attend to, the temptation. We are personally responsible for what we think, and we do have control and can think about something else if we choose. Jesus was human and was tempted as we are (see Hebrews 4:15). As a human, Jesus was also subject to the limitations of serial processing. It is actually this limitation that provides the best explanation of why Jesus did not know when he would return, which is a troublesome passage to some (see Matthew 24:36). He simple chose not to attend to that information. As evidence that Jesus had this limitation we can see Him utilizing it during His temptations. When Jesus was tempted, what did He do? He quoted Scripture. But, not just any Scripture; Jesus quoted specific Scripture that opposed the temptation. He attended to His Father's truth that opposed His enemy's lies. Satan said, "Turn this stone into bread" (Luke 4:3), and Jesus responded, "Man does not live by bread alone" (Luke 4:4), and therein He meditated on the truth that He was both physical and spiritual and that He was sent to do the sole will of His father, not that of Satan. Man cannot attend to two things at the same time and Jesus chose to attend to the will of His Father. It is a truthful statement: To whatever degree light is introduced, darkness is dispelled.

Now we have to deal with James statement that the devil "will flee from you." Is it not more common that

Satan—when opposed by righteousness—simply takes a short step back, or sideways, only to immediately attack again? It is understandable that when one actively opposes Satan by attending to truth that one can no longer be attending to the temptation and evil. But "out of mind" is not the same as "out of here!" There is a distinct difference between backing off for a moment and fleeing from you, and Scripture tells us that if we resist the devil, he will flee, not just back off. Let's re-examine the temptations of Jesus. Scripture tells us that at the beginning of Jesus' ministry and after Jesus came out of the wilderness, Satan tempted Jesus three times. Each temptation focused on one of the three "ways" of temptation. Jesus resisted the three temptations by opposing the temptations with truth. What did Satan do? That's correct, he left Jesus for a more "opportune time" (see Luke 4:13). So at least for a time, he went away or fled. To understand the power of Scripture against Satan and the principles that will make Satan flee, one must understand how God designed humans to learn.

How people learn is an area of study that interests educators and psychologists. Researchers have identified a number of specific styles of learning, from simple observation to the manner in which we respond to reward, punishers and complex associations. The single thing all these learning theories have in common is they function by forming associations (or relationships). So humans, at the most basic level, learn through association. As discussed earlier, even brains are specifically structured to maximize learning through association. Psychology is a social science and most of the principles in psychology contain exceptions to the rule. Because of the nature of social sciences, most principles are stated in terms of tendencies or probabilities. Associative learning is founded in a law, rather than a tendency or probability. The "law of contiguity" states that when two stimuli (in this case the stimuli are thoughts) are paired together, they will become a learned association. It is not a principle or a probability; it is a law. One psychological intervention based on associative learning and its corresponding law of contiguity is systematic desensitization and systematic desensitization, while it may take some time, is always effective when correctly applied. Systematic desensitization is a behavioral intervention and one of the therapies that the American Psychological Association lists as an Empirically Supported Treatment. So what is the characteristic that provides for a law and elevates this particular treatment to complete effectiveness? The answer lies in the saying of the neuroscientist; "neurons that fire together, wire together." That is what is occurring through these associations and that is why it can be elevated to a law - it is physiological in nature. Some associations require a single pairing, while other associations require multiple pairings. The point is that we have much control of what is associated.

Associative learning was originally called classical conditioning and focused on behaviors that were reflexive in nature. As researchers began to realize that these associations could include stimuli other than those that are reflexive in nature the name gradually changed to associative learning. In his original experiments, Ivan Pavlov, demonstrated this learning association with a dog's reflexive salivation response. Pavlov paired a tone from a tuning fork with ground and dried meat powder that was puffed into the dog's mouth so that it contacted the mucus membrane. The contact of the meat powder on the mucus membrane inside the dog's mouth caused a reflexive response of salivation. After a number of pairings of the tone and meat powder, Pavlov discovered he could sound the tone from the tuning fork and the dog would begin to salivate before the meat powder could be introduced. Today, we refer this learned response as an anticipatory response. A simple way to understand these paired associations and the resulting learning that occurs is to assign the numbers 1, 2 and 3 to each stage. Once learning occurs the 1-2-3 becomes 1 to 3. Applied to Pavlov's experiment it would look like this. The tone is 1, the puff of meat powder onto the mucus membrane of the dog's mouth is 2 and the salivation response is 3. So a pairing would be 1-tone, 2-meat powder and 3-salivation. Once learning occurs, which is more specifically a new firing of the neurons, 1-2-3 becomes 1 to 3 so the 1-tone leads straight to 3-salivation. The process whereby the neurons build their new wiring is attributed to the human minds tendency to function parsimoniously, or in as simple a manner as possible. In other words, once a number of pairings occur the brain figures out it can bypass 2 and go straight from 1 to 3 by creating a new neural pathway. (See figure 7-2.)

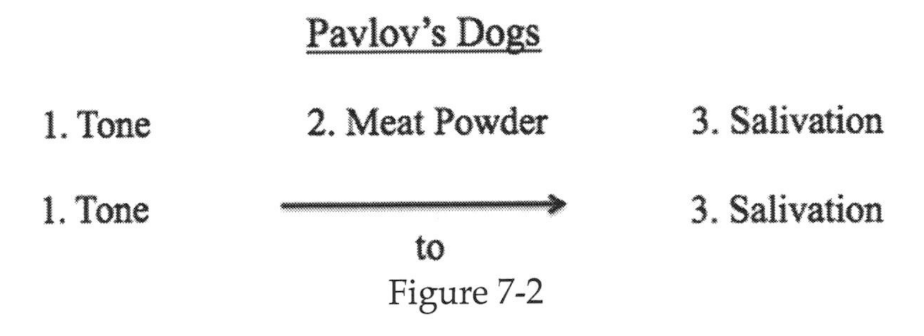

Figure 7-2

Every reader of this book has been subject to the effects of associative learning. Have you ever eaten a specific food, and then unfortunately discovered you had a stomach virus that led to one or more undesirable symptoms? I think most people have experienced this scenario that psychologists call acquired taste aversion. This learning process includes 1-food, 2-stomach virus and 3-undesirable symptoms. Once learning occurs the 1-2-3 becomes 1 to 3 so the 1-food you ate just before you became ill now causes 3-nausea if you even think about it. We had pizza for dinner the night my wife went into labor with our fourth child. She didn't have a stomach virus, however we can safely assume labor leads to the same end result of nausea and a pairing of pizza and nausea occurred with my wife. It was six months before the kids and I could even talk about how much we missed eating pizza around my wife and another six months before we could actually bring it into the house. (See figure 7-3.)

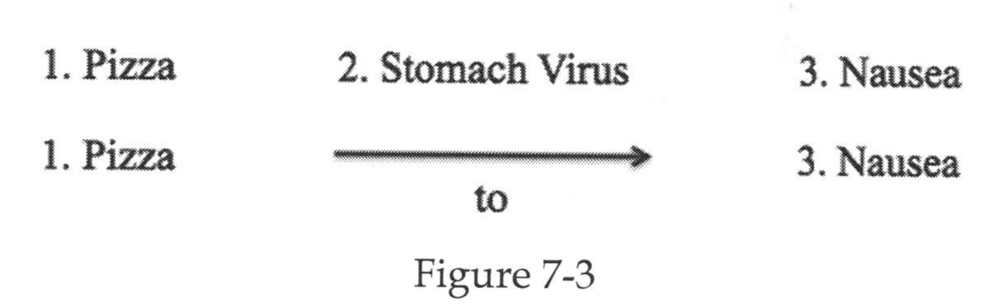

Figure 7-3

Sometimes the learning is subtler and not readily evident. I've illustrated the subtle nature of associative learning with my classes with the following example. As I walk into class I make the following statement. "I want everyone to clear your desk, get out a plain piece of paper and write your name in the top, right hand corner." I then wait for the students to complete the task and when they are all sitting quietly with their papers on their desks I continue. "I now want each of you to find your pulse on your wrist and using the clock in the front of the room count how many heartbeats you have in one minute. Once you have that number, write it on the paper." Within a few minutes each has completed that task. I then tell them to get out their notebooks and I begin the day's lecture. About thirty minutes later, I stop the lecture and tell them to find their pulse and again count their heartbeats per minute.

I then have them write this number down and we do a quick average of the first sample of beats per minute that we took at the beginning of class and the second sample just taken. The difference is amazing as you might expect. Why? Because students have associated cleared desks and a plain piece of paper with a name in the top right hand corner with quizzes and quizzes lead to anxiety. I didn't say we were going to have a quiz. I even told them the first day of class I did not give pop quizzes. Regardless, the plain piece of paper has a profound effect on their anxiety levels and their heart rates. (See figure 7-4.) I had a student come up after class one day and ask, "I have a friend that is really funny and always makes me laugh. I've noticed that now, just the sight of him, actually just the thought of him, makes me laugh. Is this associative learning?" "You are a fast learner." I replied.

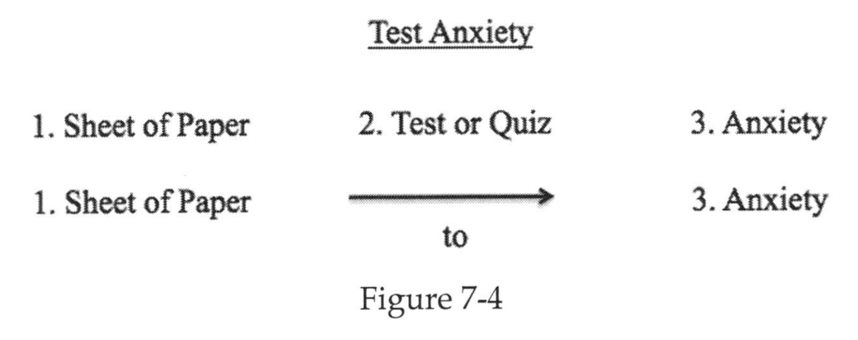

Figure 7-4

Temptation is designed by Satan to lead to sin, and meditating on the Word of God leads to righteousness. When Jesus was tempted, He consistently associated Satan's temptation to Scripture. If we consistently pair Satan's temptations with God's truth, learning will occur through new associations, and at some point the temptation will actually lead to righteous thoughts. That bears repeating. Satan's temptation will lead to righteous thoughts! It is a certainty because it is founded on the law of contiguity. Of course, the last thing Satan wants is for anyone to associate his evil and darkness with God's truth and light. At some point he will "flee from you," because he does not want his deceptions to lead to righteousness. (See Figure 7-5.)

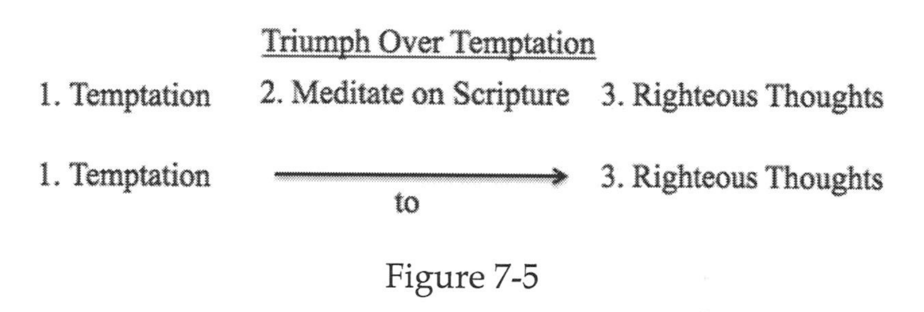

Figure 7-5

Finally, God tells us that He is faithful and will always provide an escape from temptation (see 1 Corinthians 10:13). Referring back to my temptation, you are probably wondering if I stole the cheese? Well, the whole time I was reasoning to do evil, I was standing on a fallen tree stump that jutted out over an icy, mountain lake. You can probably fill in the rest of the story. I'll just tell you I never had a chance to steal the cheese and, no, I still don't think falling into that lake was God's plan of escape for me. What is the escape provided by God? Jesus' escape came in the form of the truth of Scripture. Is it not probable that God has provided a truth, through His word, that could be used to oppose any of Satan's deceptions we may ever deal with? Is this the escape provided by God?

The first client I counseled was a single mother completing her nursing degree and working at the hospital associated with the university I attended. She was facing the stressful approach of final exams and graduation – if the exams went well. She had experienced her first panic attack on the cardiac care floor where she worked. The doctors ran some tests, concluded that she was having panic attacks and sent her to the universities psychological services clinic where I was doing my supervised training. She had two distinct panic attacks within the first half hour of our first session and I felt the need to take a fifteen-minute break. "Taking a break" was code at the clinic and meant that the counselor in training needed to consult with a supervisor. I was troubled by my client's situation and I really wanted to do something to help her gain control so she could complete her exams and graduate. When I entered the room where the supervisors watched the various counseling sessions transpire on closed circuit television, one of the supervisors motioned for me to sit down next to him. He had been watching the session and asked me what my thoughts were regarding the situation. I communicated my desire to help my client gain control quickly and he said, "I believe thought stopping might do the trick." To that I replied with something like, "that sounds like an excellent approach. Now remind me what that is exactly?" As he reviewed the technique I began to recall the details so we quickly formulated a plan.

I returned to the office where my client was seated and told her that she probably believed that the panic attacks had total control over her. What I wanted to do was empower her with a technique whereby she could control the panic. Her facial expression communicated a lack of confidence as I continued. I told her to close her eyes and to call out a number that corresponded to her level of anxiety. The number one would represent normal anxiety and the number ten would represent a full-blown panic attack. I told her that I wanted her to try to experience another panic attack if possible. She closed her eyes and I immediately asked her for a number. She called out "six." A moment later she called out "eight" - then "nine" - and finally "ten." Her breathing was labored and her face showed the same concern it had expressed during the first two panic attacks. Her eyes were still closed and I knew I only had a moment to act. I quickly leaned toward her and with as much volume as I could muster I yelled "STOP!" right in her face as I simultaneously clapped my hands as loud as I could. She screamed as her body flailed rearward and her eyes opened wide. I quickly said, "Give me a number." She replied with a confused, "What?" I repeated my statement, "Give me a number." It registered this time, she thought for a moment and replied, "panic one - fear ten!" By demonstrating that she could control the panic attacks I offered hope. We talked about what she could do when she left the clinic and we decided that each time she felt a panic attack coming on she would close her eyes and within her imagination she would yell "STOP" and let the imagined sound reverberate in her head. We met for three consecutive evenings following our first session. She had two difficult days, however, she began to experience a comfortable level of control by the third day. She did not return for any more sessions. I later found out that my supervisor had asked one of the doctors she worked with, one that was there when she had her first panic attack, how she was doing. He said she had returned to work within a couple days, she had graduated and she was working full time at the hospital.

In the twenty years that have followed my first attempt at implementing thought stopping, I have come to understand that thought stopping can stop panic attacks, but that is all. Christians are to live by faith and a mature faith requires one to will and act according to God's good purpose. More specifically, a mature faith is motivated by love and includes the development of goodness, knowledge, self-control and perseverance to produce the fruit of the Spirit. Opposing, and thereby associating, the world's deception with God's truth leads to righteous thoughts. The world may have a way of controlling anxiety but God can transform us from the inside out and make us a peace tree that actually bears the fruit of peace.

When I work with clients suffering with panic attacks or other forms of severe anxiety, at some point we will search God's word for truths that can oppose whatever deceptions they are facing. In cases where my client is dealing with anxiety, we often settle in on a passage from Philippians to oppose the fear creating the anxiety. Paul writes,

> [4]"Rejoice in the Lord always. I will say it again: Rejoice! [5]Let your gentleness be evident to all. The Lord is near. [6]Do not be anxious about anything, but in everything, by prayer and petition, with thanksgiving, present your requests to God. [7]And the peace of God, which transcends all understanding, will guard your hearts and your minds in Christ Jesus. [8]Finally, brothers, whatever is true, whatever is noble, whatever is right, whatever is pure, whatever is lovely, whatever is admirable — if anything is excellent or praiseworthy — think about such things. [9]Whatever you have learned or received or heard from me, or seen in me — put it into practice. And the God of peace will be with you." (Philippians 4:4-9.)

I usually educate my client regarding the basic premises of "putting off by putting on," typically providing only as much information as needed to foster an attitude of hope. I explain that allowing the Scripture to really speak to them personally, in their time of need, is of utmost importance. While I provide them with an overview of possible directions in which the Scripture might direct their thoughts, I encourage them to augment my ideas with their own personal insights. Focusing on aspects of Scripture that are most relevant to their specific fears will effectively equip them to oppose the deceptions.

I'll briefly share some of the thoughts that might get discussed in a typical counseling session. I may begin by reminding her that God loves her more than she can imagine and that God has given her His Spirit to strengthen her and his Word to guide her. She knows this already (see 2 Peter 1:12), however she has likely lost sight of these truths due to her preoccupation with the anxiety and fear. Recalling these truths should begin to rekindle her attitude of joy (verse 4). After, reminding her of the love that God has for her and attempting to generate a healthier attitude, I'll begin to introduce knowledge relevant to her anxiety. We discuss the way that anxiety focuses internally on self and how Christian love is to focus externally on others. An inordinate self-focus both initiates and facilitates anxiety. This may well be one of the areas where she has deviated from the will of God. The body of research on mental health in general informs us that there is a strong positive correlation between self-focus and psychopathology. God intends that we rely on Him to meet our needs as we busy ourselves with meeting the needs of others. First John 4:18 tells us that, "Perfect love drives out fear" and Paul specifically speaks to the importance of focusing externally by demonstrating compassion to others when we are dealing with fear and anxiety by instructing us to let our "gentleness be evident to all" (verse 7). The term "gentleness" here refers to one's Christ-like affection for others. (I wonder if this perfect love, experienced in its purest form in heaven, would possess such a strong external focus that one would be unaware of one's body? Paul may have contemplated this same thing as he wrote in 2 Corinthians 12:2, "I know a man in Christ who fourteen years ago was caught up to the third heaven. Whether it was in the body or out of the body I do not know – God knows.") I may encourage my client to compare the proper external focus of Christian love with her current thoughts and behaviors and to note the contrast. She will probably discover that her service to others has diminished in direct proportion to her experienced anxiety. Once we have begun to generate a healthier Christian attitude and identified what she should be thinking and doing (knowledge), we begin to reason how she can begin to exercise self-control and put these things into practice.

I'll explain that exercising self-control will take two forms as she begins to engage in new thoughts and new actions. First, when she begins to experience the onset of her symptoms, she will exercise self-control as she directs her thoughts to, and begins to meditate on, the ideas we are exploring from Philippians 4. In addition, she will begin to actively identify and pursue opportunities to serve others in Christian love. These two new ways of thinking and acting will oppose the anxiety and fear and begin to create new, healthier associations between the fear and a proper reliance on God to overcome that fear. Finally, we will project into the future and discuss any difficulties she believes she may face in implementing this plan (perseverance). As we discuss the attitude she should adopt as she engages this fight within, a fight between good and evil, I may introduce a passage from James for further instruction and encouragement. James writes,

> "[2]Consider it pure joy, my brothers, whenever you face trials of many kinds, [3]because you know that the testing of your faith develops perseverance. [4]Perseverance must finish its work so that you may be mature and complete, not lacking anything. [5]If any of you lacks wisdom, he should ask God, who gives generously to all without finding fault, and it will be given to him." (James 1:2-5)

James tells us that when we face trials we are literally at a fork in the road. In her case anxiety is the impulsive, easy route (walking by sight) and because it is so laden with emotion, it has distracted her attention away from the alternative (walking by faith). It is important that she acknowledge the fact that there is another path that can and should be taken. Not only that, she should have an attitude of joy because this fork in the road provides her with an opportunity to begin a new pattern, a new association, which will strengthen her faith and enable her to overcome. Each new opportunity to choose the correct path should be viewed with an attitude of joy.

Finally, we will discuss the necessity of prayer to her growth and maturation. James instructs us to pray for wisdom and encourages us to expect to receive what we pray for (verse 5). John also speaks to the confidence we can have when we ask God for things we need to grow spiritually. John writes, "This is the confidence we have in approaching God: that if we ask anything according to his will, he hears us. And if we know that he hears us - whatever we ask - we know that we have what we asked of him" (1 John 5:14, 15). God desires that His children have the necessities to live in peace. If we pray for something we know that God has told us he wants us to have, he hears us and we have what we asked. We do not know when we will receive it or in what measure, but we can be confident it will be at just the right time in just the right amount. We then discuss some of the things it would be helpful to pray for given the situation at hand and I'll typically say a prayer on her behalf. I might pray; "Dear Lord, I am here with one of your children who has been distracted by the evils of this world. You know what she is dealing with and you know her heart. I ask you to rekindle the joy that comes from being your child, a joy she has known in the past. Remind her that you are here for her and you love her dearly. When the deceptions of the world try to force their way into her mind, fill her with truth and light and dispel all the darkness of evil. Motivate her to love others as you love her and make her a peace tree that bears the fruit of love, joy and peace. I pray these things in the name of Jesus. Amen."

CHAPTER 8

CHRISTIAN ONE-ANOTHERING

Toward the conclusion of chapter one I listed Robert's five key elements that he believes are typical of what a Christian psychology might include. In this chapter we will focus on Robert's fifth key element: psychotherapy. Roberts (1997) states, "A psychology need not actually include a psychotherapy–a set of interventions that aim to correct or prevent unhealthy patterns of interaction and traits of personality–but the development of one is natural, and psychologies that arise out of the practices of life can be expected to have at least a rudimentary therapy" (pp. 76, 77). The human soul is defined by its relationships, and internal soul relationships are a representation of an external reality. When one takes on the role of counselor, one actually takes on a role of facilitator of external relationships that will potentially redefine the soul of another.

As Christians, we are all called to show the love of Christ to others. As such, we facilitate the redefining of souls by "speaking the truth in love" (Ephesians 4:15) so others may grow in their faith. While the main focus of this chapter will be an exploration into a facilitative, Christian one-anothering relationship, I begin with a few observations, within the context of relationships that define the soul, concerning secular theories of psychotherapy and other facilitative relationships.

Secular Theories of Psychotherapy

You may recall the fable from India of the blind men and the elephant. Each described the elephant in relation to the part he first touched. The blind man who touched the side claimed that the elephant was like a wall. The blind man who touched the tail stated that the elephant was like a rope. On and on the fable went, with each blind man defining the animal by what he felt. Each blind man was correct; yet, each only experienced a small part of the whole elephant. This fable provides a good analogy for psychology as a science attempting to understand God's human creation. Each piece of information gleaned through psychological research has the potential to be a little piece of the human creation puzzle. As stated earlier, we should not totally reject secular causal factors of pathology, because they may be implicated as a cause of despair, inasmuch as they constitute a deviation from the will of God. Every man has access to the general revelation of God's creation that demonstrates His power and His order. However, trying to decipher or discern which pieces are Scripturally valid and which are erroneous can be a daunting task.

There is a scientific method, a type of heuristic, which relies on convergent validity that I have often found valuable to gaining insight. This method involves a process wherein every piece of information within a specific set of parameters is examined to see what all the pieces may have in common. If a pattern is identified, attention is broadened to other areas of study to see if there is agreement with our original pattern. If the interdisciplinary perspectives are in agreement with our original pattern, the information converges to augment our understanding of the finding. At one point in my doctoral research I did this with more than twenty prominent theories of psychotherapy. Through that research, I discovered a basic structure all those theories had in common, a structure with three component parts connected by three relationships. The component parts of each theory include the therapist, the client, and the goals of that particular therapeutic model. The structural component parts and relationships are diagrammed in figure 8-1 and should appear familiar to the reader.

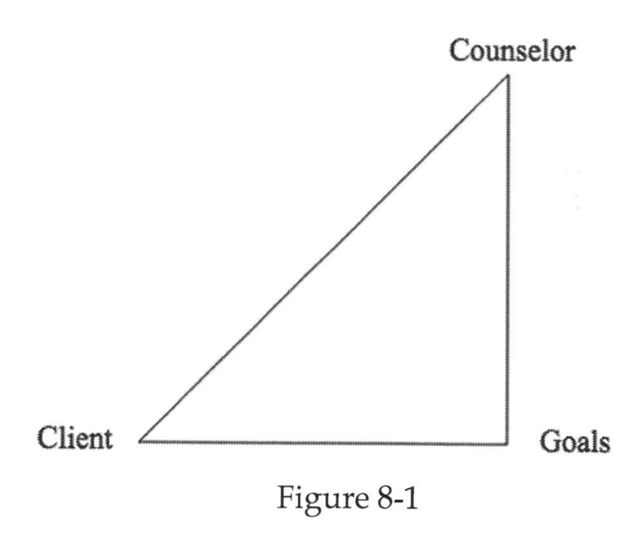

Figure 8-1

A client dealing with a problem that is creating a motivating level of discomfort enters into a helping relationship with a counselor. The client hopes that the counselor has built a relationship, through academics or experience, with some idea or concept that will remedy the client's problem. This idea or concept represents the goal of the counseling relationship, and this goal is grounded in its source. If the counselor is using a theory of psychotherapy in its pure form, the goal is grounded in the originator of the psychotherapy. The counselor in this case is functioning as a representative facilitator for the psychotherapeutic model. If the therapist has modified the theory of psychotherapy, as do eclectic counselors, the goal is additionally grounded in the counselor to the degree that the therapy has been modified. Through the counselor-client relationship, the problem is clarified, and a tentative goal is established within the context of the specific theory of psychotherapy. This goal, it is hoped, will remedy the client's problem and relieve the discomfort. Once the goal is identified, the client must make a decision to build a personal relationship with that goal. That relationship is formed through insight or action, or both insight and action.

It is typical for a recipient to build a faith relationship by first gaining new knowledge and then transferring the newly acquired knowledge into new and more appropriate ways of behaving. So their relationship with the goal develops through both insight and action. As facilitators, it is normal to both educate and encourage. While it is a rare occurrence, we sometimes discover that newly acquired information is sufficient to lift a person out of despair. In these cases insight is all that is necessary. A young woman sat in my office on the occasion of her first appointment and proceeded to tell me about her difficulties. Deeply troubled and with tears in her eyes she told me that her mother had unexpectedly passed away six months previous and she was concerned because her grieving did not appear to be getting easier. She told me that her mother was her best friend, that she dearly missed her and that she often cried herself to sleep at night. She knew that grieving was normal, however, she was deeply concerned because she believed that the intensity of her grief, six months after her mother's passing, was not normal. There are indeed cases where people develop an unhealthy pathological grief, however, she did not meet the criteria. I then provided her with information she needed. I told her that research on grieving demonstrated that what she was experiencing was normal. I told her that in the United States, intense grieving normally lasts from three months to a year and profound grieving can last as long as three years. Immediately her eyes brightened and a look of peace came over her. As she rose out of her chair she thanked me and said, "I guess that's all I needed" and she was gone. I didn't even have a chance to ask her if there was anything else we could talk about. I vividly recall that situation because it was a simple problem with a simple solution. It is very common to see a client experience an "aha!" moment when new information leads to insight. It is not all that common for the insight alone to be sufficient.

While the focus of this book is on the development of a Christian psychology, it will be beneficial for the reader if we briefly examine a specific secular theory of psychotherapy in the context of the relationship triad seen in figure 8-1. We will consider this relationship triad as nonspecific, because we are not viewing the triad in a context of spiritual or worldly. Instead, we are considering it solely based on its component parts and connecting relationships. Sigmund Freud's Psychoanalytic theory will serve as our example, as it was the first comprehensive secular theory of psychotherapy. While many of Freud's views are in direct opposition to Scripture, it is possible that we would not even be discussing a Christian psychology at this point in history had Freud not laid the groundwork. As such, researchers in the field find that— though they may not in any way identify with Freud—they are indeed "post-Freudian" in that they are challenging a paradigm he originally defined. You may recall that this theory was mentioned in the first chapter as one that is widely practiced even though it lacks empirical support. It would be helpful to the reader to refer to figure 8-2, as we progress through our example.

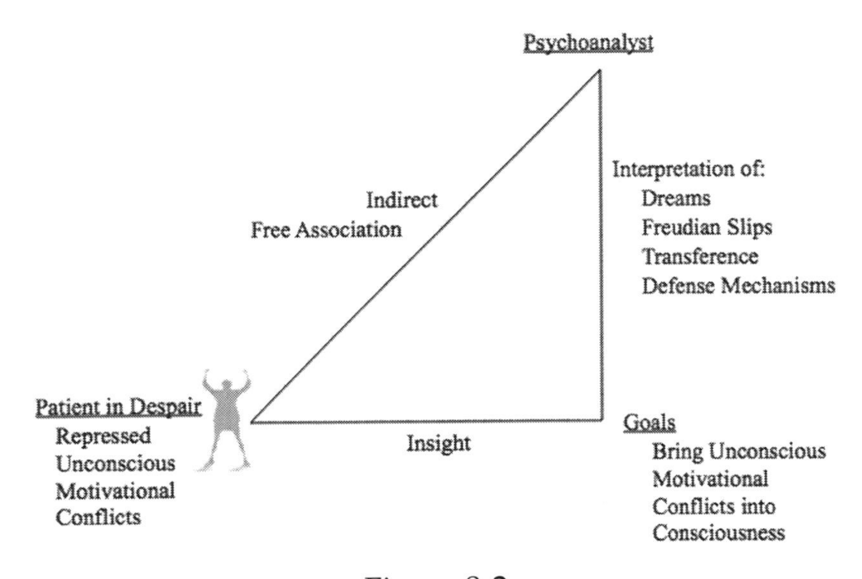

Figure 8-2

According to Psychoanalytic theory, an individual (patient) experiences pathology (despair) because of repressed, unconscious motivational conflicts between the id and the superego (personality structures), or what Sigmund Freud originally called the "it" and the "upper-I". Typically, the id desires something that the superego assesses as unacceptable, and a conflict between the two opposing parts of the psyche ensues. If not reconciled, the resulting motivational conflict will be repressed into the unconscious. The number and magnitude of the repressed, unconscious motivational conflicts directly influence the level of despair experienced by the patient. The goal of therapy, according to psychoanalytic theory, is to bring the repressed, unconscious motivational conflicts into consciousness. This is accomplished when the psychoanalyst accurately identifies the unconscious motivational conflicts, and the patient acknowledges their existence (insight). The psychoanalyst facilitates the process of identifying the unconscious motivational conflicts (goals) by encouraging the patient to engage in free association wherein the patient talks about whatever comes to mind. Freud believed that free association increased the volatility of the unconscious motivational conflicts. This disturbance within the unconscious caused the patient to manifest conflicts through transference, Freudian slips, defense mechanisms, and dreams that were then interpreted by the psychoanalyst. The psychoanalyst remains neutral in the relationship to encourage free association and the development of transference. In essence, the patient is placing hope in the technique of free association and the interpretation of transference, dreams, defense mechanisms, and Freudian slips to identify the unconscious motivational conflicts that are causing the patient to despair. Once the psychoanalyst identifies and interprets the unconscious motivational conflict, the patient experiences insight, and the unconscious conflict is released into consciousness. (Refer back to figure 8-2.)

It is a fairly simple task to assign the component parts and identify the relationships for all theories of psychotherapy according to this nonspecific triad. Actually doing so is an excellent way to organize the various theories of psychotherapy. It also demonstrates how man searches for answers within the relationship framework established by God. Our purpose, however, is to augment our understanding of the relationship triad. To this end we will continue with the heuristic and move outside the field of psychotherapy to examine other facilitative relationships.

All Facilitative Relationships

While a sound argument could be made that all personal interactions are facilitative in that they are need-motivated and goal-oriented, we will limit our focus to a few relationships where these characteristics are obvious. As we broaden our perspective beyond the counseling relationship, we discover that parenting, teaching, preaching, and discipling are similar relationships in that they are goal-oriented, and in that a person serves as a facilitator to help another reach those goals. As such, each relationship fits our nonspecific triad. (See figure 8-3.)

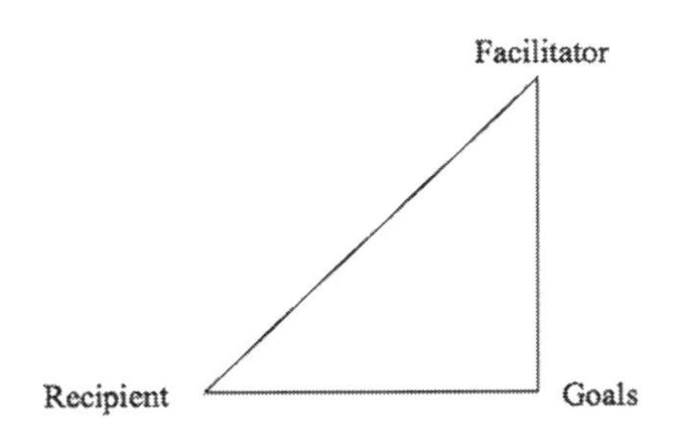

Facilitator	Recipient	Goals
Counselor	Client	Goals of Psychotherapy
Parent	Child	Social & Christian Maturity
Teacher	Student	Course Objectives
Preacher	Church Member	Christian Maturity
Discipler	Disciple	Christian Maturity

Figure 8-3

The primary criticism leveled against the development of a Christian psychology is that the Bible does not specifically address the counseling relationship. That is true, because the Bible is actually a guide for all Christian facilitative relationships of which counseling is only one. The primary characteristics that differentiate these facilitative relationships are the duration of the relationship and the specificity of the goals. Parenting and discipling, for instance, have an open-ended duration and goals that are constantly redefined as the recipient (child or disciple) matures. Teaching, as in classroom instruction, has a specific duration and a more narrowly defined set of goals referred to as course objectives. Finally, counseling has a limited duration and goals with a common characteristic: that which is necessary to bring a person out of despair.

Christian One-Anothering

As we move into a discussion of Christian one-anothering, we reflect on the testimonial in chapter four. The testimonial illustrated that man begins as recipient of God's love and then naturally moves into a position where he assumes the role of facilitator of God's love as he shares the joy he has found with others. Think about the testimonial. First, our speaker was the recipient of God's love and his soul began to be transformed or redefined by new, spiritual relationships. When he began to walk with Christ and live by faith, he took on a new role, one of facilitator. Becoming a facilitator and going to the top of the spiritual triad to act on behalf of God is part of God's plan. Paul wrote, "We are therefore Christ's ambassadors, as though God were making his appeal through us. We implore you on Christ's behalf: Be reconciled to God" (2 Corinthians 5:20). Jesus Himself commanded us to go into the entire world as His ambassadors (see Mark 16:15). As ambassadors, we demonstrate the love that God has for us to others, and we build a one-anothering relationship in Christian love. Being in relationship with Christ, we live by faith. A life of faith produces the fruit of the Spirit, and the first attribute of that fruit mentioned in Galatians 5:11 is love. Paul reinforces this faith-love relationship by stating; "The only thing that counts is faith expressing itself through love" (Galatians 5:6b). (See figure 8-4.)

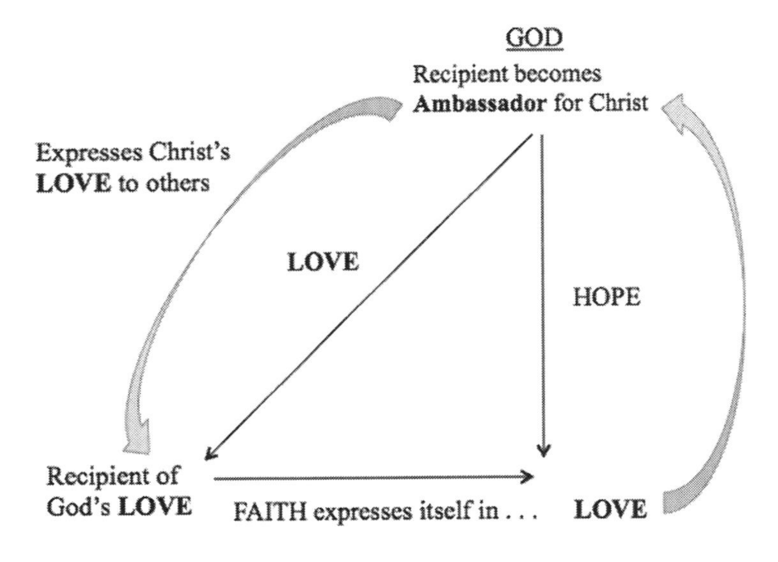

Figure 8-4

Of course, there is an alternative. If one can serve as ambassador for Christ, one can alternatively serve as an ambassador for Satan and the world. Jesus Himself said, "He who is not with me is against me" (Matthew 12:30a). Many theories of psychotherapy are founded on beliefs that are in direct opposition to Scripture, and, therefore, they are rooted in the worldly relationship triad. These theories are grounded in their respective psychotherapies, and the therapists are facilitators for the world. They encourage people to define themselves by worldly standards or things less than God. "They are from the world and therefore speak from the viewpoint of the world, and the world listens to them" (1 John 4:5). Sadly enough, many of these worldly theories appear acceptable to many Christians. The only accurate way to discern what is from God and what is from Satan and the world is to have a keener understanding of the relationship characteristics in both the spiritual and worldly triad. For this reason alone, the necessity of developing a Christian psychology cannot be understated.

I use the term "one-anothering" to signify facilitative relationships we encounter as Christians, as ambassadors for Christ. In Scripture, the one-another commands lay the foundation for Christian relationships. These direct commands guide our attitudes, thoughts, and actions as we relate to others. Spiritual one-anothering implies a reliance on the Word of God and the work of the Holy Spirit in the helping relationship. Referring to the helping relationship as "psychotherapy" implies a reliance on psychological theories and methods. When we assume the role of ambassador for Christ Jesus, we speak only what pleases Christ, just as He spoke only what pleased His Father in heaven (see John 5:19). As ambassadors for Christ, we are "speaking the truth in love" (Ephesians 4:25). The relationship we build with one another reflects, as much as is humanly possible through the work of the Holy Spirit, the relationship God has with us. We love with Christ's love, focusing on the needs of the individual and acting in some way to meet those needs (see Philippians 4:5).

One-Anothering in the Spiritual Triad

We continue by examining one-anothering within the context of the relationships that define the parameters of the human soul. While a complete text could be dedicated to this topic, we will limit this discussion to a few basic observations. We begin by examining one-anothering in the context of the three relationships that make up the spiritual triad. (See figure 8-5.)

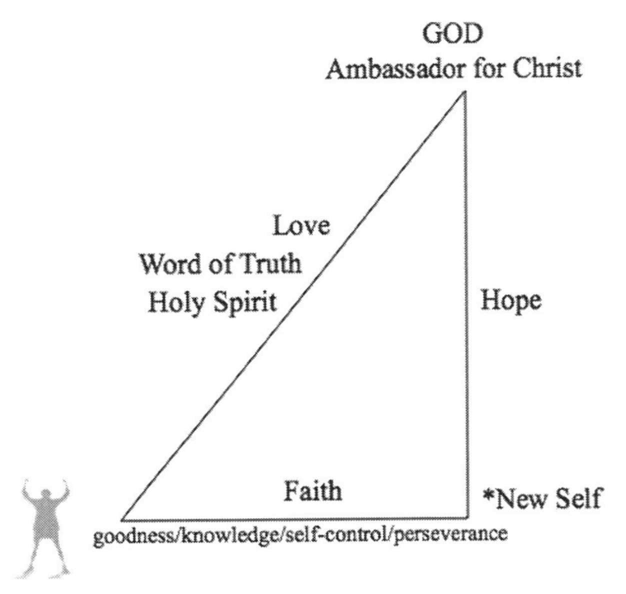

*Products of faith: love, joy, peace, patience, kindness, goodness, faithfulness, gentleness, self-control (Gal. 5:22, 23).

Figure 8-5

When we enter into a facilitative, one-anothering relationship, we acknowledge that we are ambassadors for Christ. As such, we will encourage others to redefine themselves in relation to God and His directives for their lives. The ties that bind our relationship with another are, therefore, grounded in God. As we consider the three relational ties that bind us as individuals to God (love, truth, and the Holy Spirit), we acknowledge that, as ambassadors for Christ, they are the same ties that bind us in relationships with others. We are motivated to act as ambassadors for Christ by the love that Christ has demonstrated to us personally. Likewise, we love others with a Christ-like love that focuses away from self and toward them to accurately identify their needs. This Christ-like love then moves us to compassion, and it acts in some way to meet that need and encourage others to live by faith. Just as we are enabled by the Word of Truth to know how to live within the will of God, we enable them to live by faith through that same truth. Simply stated, we act as ambassadors for Christ by "speaking the truth in love" (Ephesians 4:25). Finally, just as we are empowered by the work of the Holy Spirit in our lives to come into relationship with Christ and subsequently grow in Christ, we rely on the work of the Holy Spirit to empower others in a similar way. We acknowledge that we are "field laborers" and that it is God who, through the work of the Holy Spirit, supernaturally reconciles others to Himself through Christ Jesus and brings about Christian maturity (see 1 Corinthians 3:6-9). Just as we are motivated by love, enabled by the Word of Truth, and empowered by the Holy Spirit to act on Christ's behalf, the recipient of our one-anothering relationship must be motivated by love, enabled by the Word of Truth, and empowered by the Holy Spirit to be reconciled to God and live within His will. We have the hope that this can be accomplished because Jesus, through His blood, made it possible to come into a relationship with God and live within His will through grace. When I consider the distinctions of a Christian psychology compared to a secular psychology I often am reminded of another quote attributed to Albert Einstein. "One of mankind's greatest problems is a perfection of means and a confusion of ends." I saw that problem present itself often when I was working with secular counselors. They would get so caught up in their individual models of psychotherapy that they often would not get around to really offering anything substantive to their client to lift them out of their state of despair. This should never be the case for Christians engaged in one-anothering for God has perfected the means through Jesus Christ and specified the ends through His Word.

As we continue to build this one-anothering relationship with the recipient, we begin to focus on the individual's life of faith within the context of the problem. We recall that a living faith includes goodness, knowledge, self-control and perseverance, so we follow that guide in our relationships. We begin by assessing the state of—and developing where necessary—the individual's Christian attitude (goodness). Is he or she predisposed to desire to please God? Does each one really believe and trust God to provide direction for his or her life, and is he or she willing to submit to Him? Does the recipient believe that through God's Word, prayer, and the work of the Holy Spirit there is an escape from despair? Is this person ready to accept that–regardless of the situation–God wants to direct him or her to a better state of being? Whether it is marital problems, personal spiritual issues, or unavoidable suffering, God desires each to grow in faith and find joy. As we develop a Christian attitude, we begin to explore God's Word (knowledge) in an attempt to discover where the recipient has deviated from the will of God. As Christians we do not judge others (see Matthew 7:1). It is Jesus who judges for Jesus is the Word of Truth - the measure of man (see John 5:22). We examine thoughts, words, and deeds in the context of the problem at hand and hold each alongside the Word. What thoughts, words, or deeds are inconsistent with the standard of the regenerated soul, the new self, delineated by Scripture? Once the problem thoughts, words, or deeds are identified, we seek to discover what Biblical thoughts, words, or deeds the recipient needs to form a relationship with, because the latter cannot coexist with the former. This new information is then put into practice in the life of the individual (self-control). Finally, we encourage the person to continue (persevere) in this new way of thinking and acting, even if the results are not what were expected or desired, because the person ultimately must assess what is right not by outcome, but by what pleases God. We are confident that God will work through this process (see Romans 8:28), and we rely heavily on the power of prayer as we one-another (see 1 John 5:14 and James 1:5).

A number of years ago I sat in an Elder's meeting discussing one of those situations we would have preferred to avoid but had a Scriptural mandate to deal with. It was a situation involving new Christians and a sinful lifestyle that had to be confronted. We all knew that if the situation were not handled properly, a number of new Christians would likely leave the church - possibly forever. I realized it was a situation that I, as an Elder, a minister and a psychologist was probably best equipped to handle. I volunteered and everyone at the meeting was relieved. One of our senior Elders followed up with, "I think you ought not go by yourself." I had dealt with difficult situations by myself in the context of counseling many times, however, there was wisdom to his words and we all agreed. The senior Elder then volunteered to go with me to the meeting. He had never attended college and I don't really think he had even graduated from high school. While he didn't fit the profile of someone who might be useful in this situation, I was not concerned at all for I knew he had a good heart and a gentle, loving spirit and, after all, he was really only going as a witness. The day arrived for our meeting and we sat down with the church members to discuss the issue. I presented the problem in a loving manner and then I took on the role of listener, as I was very interested to know exactly where they were in their thinking about the subject. When they finished talking there was a little period of time where no one said anything. Extended silence is sometimes a good thing as the longer it lasts the more substantial the statement needs to be that breaks the silence. I decided to wait, my fellow Elder did not. He continued to pursue the problem and it's only solution, however, he did it in a manner that demonstrated sincere compassion for the spiritual well being of the church members. While he surely had a strong personal opinion regarding the situation, he correctly measured their actions along side Scripture. As I sat back and listened to the other Elder and the church members discuss the situation, I realized that the senior Elder was handling the situation as well, or better, than I might have. He helped them finalize a plan for accountability, we had a prayer and parted ways in Christian unity. What I had been dreading turned out to be an edifying experience for all of us and I really did not play a substantial part in the process or the outcome. I did get to see a wise Shepherd with a Christ like affection for others, well versed in Scripture, act in a way to meet the needs of his flock. The Word of God indeed equips us for every good work (see 2 Timothy 3:16, 17).

This same one-anothering process applies to other areas of our lives. We train up children in the same way, motivating by love, enabling by truth, and empowering by the work of the Spirit in their lives. We develop their attitude, help them discover God's will through the Word, encourage them to put that into practice, and continue in that life. I remember a situation where my oldest daughter Katie had behaved inappropriately and was likely going to end up being punished. When I asked her why she had acted in that particular manner she responded with, "I knew what I was doing was probably wrong, but I didn't know what else to do." Katie wanted to do what was right (goodness); she just didn't know what the right thing was (knowledge). Scripture instructs parents to "train up a child in the way they should go" (Proverbs 22:6) and I had not explained to Katie the way she should go, only the way she shouldn't go. We had a conversation about what her options might have been and she replied with, "well, that's a relief. I was really tired of doing that other thing every time!"

On another occasion all four of our girls had been bickering throughout the day. While most of the trouble was rooted in typical childish selfishness, the discord really weighed on my heart because I desired that our girls be best friends. I sat the girls down and communicated the following. "The Bible tells us that when we get to heaven we will be rewarded for all the good things we do on earth. Maybe when you get to heaven you will get a beautiful gold crown to wear. And maybe every time you do something kind for your sisters God puts a beautiful jewel in that crown. I'm really concerned because the way you girls are treating each other, I think you are probably going to be wearing one of those beat up, cardboard crowns you make in heaven without a single jewel. Why don't we all make a special effort to collect jewels for our crowns by being extra nice to each other? And by the way, the Bible tells us that if someone knows you did the kind thing, and praises you for it, that is your reward. You only get a jewel if you do the kind thing and only God sees it and we know He's always watching us." The transformation was amazing. By telling the girls of good things to come, things that offered hope for the future, they had been motivated to live their lives a little closer to the will of God. My girls love their parents and they always desire to please their parents (love gives a shove), however, on this occasion it was the hope of things to come that took them the rest of the way (hope throws a rope). A few days after my little life lesson, I stood in the hallway and watched Katie get her coloring book and crayons out for her sister Erin to use. The smile on Erin's face was worth a million dollars as she realized her older sister was actually sharing with her. I knew many of Katie's crayons would end up broken but Katie probably thought she would get an extra large jewel for this one. As Erin began to color, Katie walked out of the room and only then did she notice I had been watching her. I had a smile on my face and as Katie walked by she exclaimed, "that's an extra big jewel I just got." I replied, "That was a very nice thing you did, but I think you just lost your jewel." Now, almost twenty years later, I see our four daughters doing one kind thing after another for each other. They truly are best friends and I wonder how God will manage to get all those jewels in their crowns?

This process holds true for all forms of discipling, and it may well represent the foundational pedagogical model from which all current educational models are constructed. A teacher develops a proper attitude (goodness), disseminates relevant information (knowledge), encourages application (self-control), and, finally, requires proficiency (perseverance). At times these stages all occur within the same course, while other attitudes, information and skills are acquired over the course of one's education. I typically begin each of my class sessions attempting to create a healthy attitude in my students for the subject matter at hand. That is a fairly easy task in my introductory psychology course, which I refer to as human appreciation class, because the course is all about the students (humans) and who wouldn't like a class all about them? In courses with a counseling theme I spend time discussing the commandment to love our neighbors and the concept of one-anothering. I motivate them to learn information that may not be relevant in their immediate lives by using analogies. I may tell them in a counseling class that I'm teaching them dance moves that they need to learn because one day they are going to have to dance.

At other times, a number of these stages are strung together and I actually require them to dance. For example, in one of my courses students are required to complete an experiential project I call a "compassion journal." We spend some time discussing the characteristics of a Christ-like compassion. I explain that true compassion goes far beyond the secular concept of empathy by accurately identifying the needs of another and then doing something to meet those needs. When Jesus showed compassion it was always accompanied by action that resulted in the betterment of the individuals situation. I also explain that compassion is founded in a Christian love that focuses externally on others. Once I believe that they have a Christian attitude and biblical understanding (goodness and knowledge) of compassion I then ask them to choose a couple of people for the project with whom they interact on a regular basis. I also encourage them to pick at least one person with whom they have a difficult relationship. They then spend a week observing their normal interactions with these people. I ask them to assess how attentive they are to these people and how well they are able to identify any needs these people may have. After a week of introspection, they then begin to attempt to focus away from self and toward the others, identifying needs and acting in ways that could effectively meet those needs (self-control). I encourage them to really get out of their comfort zones as they attempt to be totally selfless in their interactions. They continue this project for five weeks (perseverance). The feedback received from students is always better than I could hope for. The majority of students convey that their relationship with their fiancé or spouse had improved dramatically and, more often than not, even the relationship they chose to include that had once been troublesome was becoming a valued relationship.

Virtually all comment that this new compassionate style of relating will be a permanent part of their future.

Faith is motivated by love, enabled by the Word of Truth and empowered by the work of the Holy Spirit. Additionally, hope motivates us to remain steadfast in our faith and to persevere. While these two motivational properties are powerful, there are additional motivational dynamics associated with the relationships that define the parameters of the soul. In the final chapter we will explore these unique motivational dynamics and examine how to utilize them as we one-another.

CHAPTER 9

MOTIVATIONAL DYNAMICS

A piece of rural wisdom says, "You can lead a horse to water, but you can't make him drink." Others add, "But you can salt his oats and sweeten the water." When we consider the organization of the relationships that define the human soul, we see that each of us is individually responsible for our own respective relationships. God loves us, but we must reciprocate that love to complete the relationship (see Revelation 3:20). Additionally, God—and one who subsequently facilitates on Christ's behalf—does not come into direct contact with a person's faith relationship. Whether or not a person builds a positive faith relationship with God's directives is ultimately a willful decision of that person. (See figure 9-1.) While God, and one who subsequently facilitates on

Christ's behalf, cannot make a person live by faith, he can encourage a person toward a positive faith relationship. As Paul stated, regarding his life of faith, it is motivated by both love and hope (see Romans 5:5 and Colossians 1:5). The salt in the oats encourages the horse to take the first drink, and the sweet water encourages the horse to continue drinking. In the same way, one chooses a life of faith when he begins to comprehend that the love of Christ focuses fully on him and that only by faith will he find hope. In other words, "Love gives a shove, and hope throws a rope!"

Figure 9-1

The motivational dynamics between the soul-defining relationships are visible in God's Word. For example, Jesus said, "If you love me, you will obey what I command" (John 14:15). So there is agreement between loving Christ and living in obedient faith. Conversely, Paul stated in 1 Corinthians 3:3 that he must address the recipients of his letter as "worldly," because they were acting in a way that was contradictory to a life of faith. Living in a worldly manner in which one is motivated by self-love, enabled by deceit, and empowered by the spirit of falsehood, is in agreement with the "acts of the sinful nature," and the "acts of the sinful nature" are produced by sight, not by faith (see Galatians 5:19). As one examines Biblical statements regarding motivational dynamics, one begins to get a better understanding of the relationships that are in agreement and the relationships that are not in agreement. Simply stated, a motivational dynamic exists if one can say that, "If relationship A exists, relationship B must exist."

While many of the motivational dynamics of the relationships that define the human soul come to be understood at an intuitive level for Christians, a more thorough understanding of these dynamics can provide a wealth of insight and guidance for anyone who facilitates on Christ's behalf. I will explain the basic principles of relationship dynamics, within the context of the relationships that define the human soul, and then I will apply the basic principles in the context of one-anothering. The application will create a cohesive rationale for the existence of counseling phenomena, such as the various forms of resistance and transference, and demonstrate that many of these phenomena can be predicted. Finally, I will apply the basic principles of relationship dynamics to the Biblical process of one-anothering.

To simplify the following insights, I will use a modified set of principles built on a collection of theories referred to as consistency theories (see Abelson *et al.*,

1968), congruity theories (see Heider, 1958), and dissonance theories (see Festinger, 1957) in the literature of psychology. These psychological theories are generically thought of as consistency theories because, in one way or another, they focus on the individual's need for consistency or agreement among beliefs. This agreement among beliefs is often referred to as "cognitive balance." Disagreement between beliefs is referred to as "cognitive dissonance." Consistency theories have three characteristics in common. First, each describes the specific conditions that must be present for beliefs to be in consistency (balance). Second, each theory asserts that inconsistency (dissonance) motivates an individual in some way to restore consistency. This restoration is motivated by an unpleasant anxiety that results from inconsistent cognitions. And third, each theory describes the means by which consistency (balance) can be regained. While we will use some basic terminology from the various consistency theories, we will allow Scripture to guide us in the proper application of that terminology.

The relationships of interest, as we attempt to better understand these relationship dynamics, include the facilitator-recipient relationship and the relationship each forms with the new-self goals of counseling. Each of these three relationships will be either positive or negative. A relationship is said to be positive if a personal, affirmative relationship is forming or has been formed. A positive, affirmative relationship is agreed with and acted on in some way. A relationship is said to be negative if no personal, affirmative relationship has been formed. Negative relationships exist when there is an absence of affirmation. The attitudes concerning a negative relationship can range from neutral to disagreement. (See figure 9-2.)

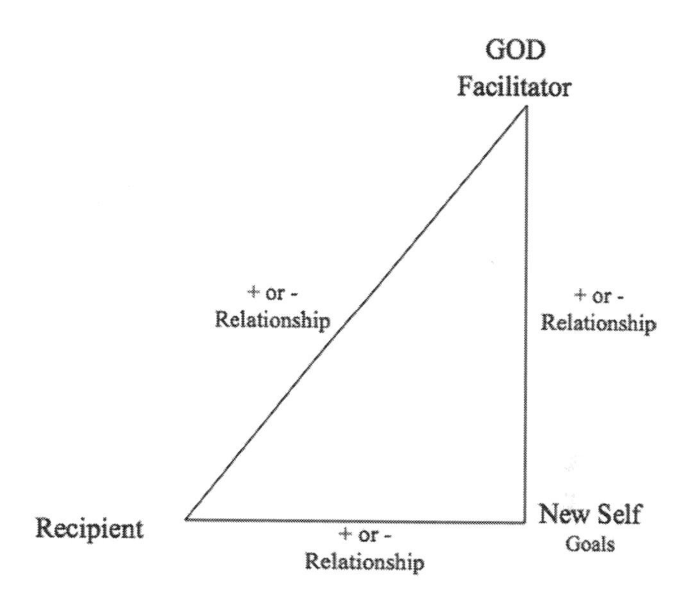

Figure 9-2

Cognitive balance (consistency) exists when there are either zero negative relationships or two negative relationships in a relationship triad. Cognitive dissonance (inconsistency) exists when there is one negative relationship in a relationship triad. Cognitive dissonance creates an uncomfortable level of anxiety that motivates a person to attempt to regain balance by manipulating relationships. While the formula sounds complex, it is really quite simple—even intuitive. An example will help to demonstrate and clarify these relationship dynamics: Carlos and Bethany have become good friends (positive relationship) over the course of their freshman year at college. Bethany's best friend Mary (positive relationship) will be coming to the school in the fall, and she will be Bethany's roommate. Bethany tells Carlos that she really hopes he likes Mary, and Carlos assures her that he will. (He infers a positive relationship.) Carlos knows that he likes Bethany and that Bethany likes Mary, so he infers a balanced set of relationships and tells her, "Any friend of yours is a friend of mine." When Mary arrives in the fall, there is an immediate personality clash between her and Carlos (negative relationship). No matter how hard they try, Carlos and Mary cannot get along. Carlos is now in a dissonant state (one negative relationship), and he is motivated to regain balance. Carlos has three options. First, he can avoid Bethany when Mary is around, thereby alleviating some of the dissonance. This is not a practical option since Mary is Bethany's best friend and roommate. The other two options involve changing one of the existing positive relationships to a negative, so the relationship triad regains balance with two negative relationships. Carlos probably desires to stay in a relationship with Bethany so he can have a heart-to-heart talk with her and present an ultimatum: "It's either me or Mary," in an attempt to create a negative relationship between her and her friend. If this does not bring the desired results of creating a negative relationship between Bethany and Mary, he will be motivated to break off his relationship with Bethany altogether. This will create a negative relationship between he and Bethany and bring balance to the relationship triad. (See figure 9-3.)

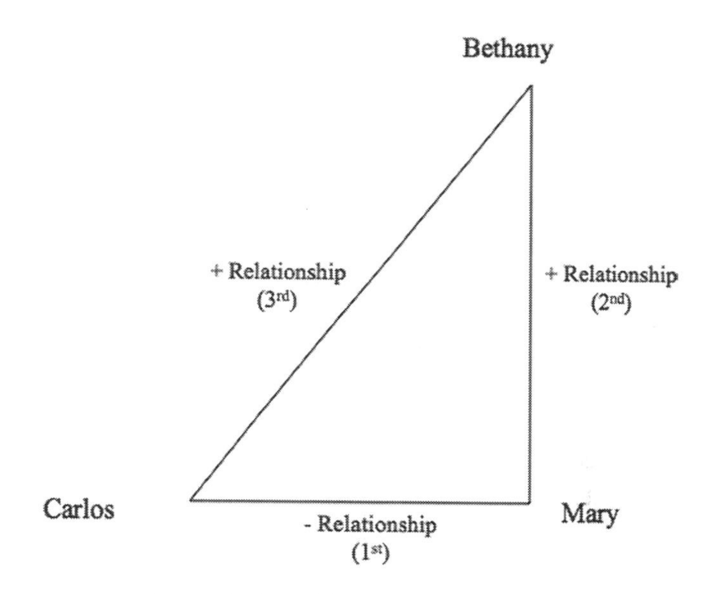

Figure 9-3

You may have witnessed this scenario, and you may well have even been a member of such a relationship triad. I have seen many dissonant relationships in counseling, often between spouses and either a friend or relative as the third entity of the relationship triad. While this example deals with a relationship triad between three individuals, the same principles apply to a relationship triad between two individuals and a goal. People are most compatible when they agree on the major issues of life and therefore experience consonant relationships. When disagreement concerning a major life issue occurs, and the issue is significant to the relationship, dissonance is experienced and each tries to convince the other to adopt their view. If one does not change opinions regarding the major life issue, the personal relationship will suffer or cease to exist. As

Christians, the single major life issue for us to agree on is the Word of God. Therefore, our unity is in Truth.

As we move to a one-anothering context, we will revisit the basic facilitative relationship triad illustrated in figure 9-2. The first thing to note as we consider this relationship triad is that God's directives constitute the new-self goals of the spiritual relationship triad, and God always has a positive relationship with His directives. God is in complete agreement with His directives, and, thus, a facilitator, acting as a responsible ambassador for Christ, is likewise in complete agreement with those directives. So the God/facilitator relationship with the new-self goals is always positive. In the same way, God's relationship with man is also positive. God loves us and desires that all men be reconciled to Him and live within His will. It is up to the facilitator, acting as ambassador, to demonstrate this Christ-like love to the recipient. By creating a Christ-like relationship with the recipient, the facilitator creates a motivational push within the recipient toward the goal. By demonstrating that the goal is grounded in God and provides hope, the facilitator creates a motivational pull within the recipient toward the goal. The two positive relationships encourage the recipient to balance (zero negatives) the relationship triad by building an affirmative faith relationship with the goals. (See figure 9-4.)

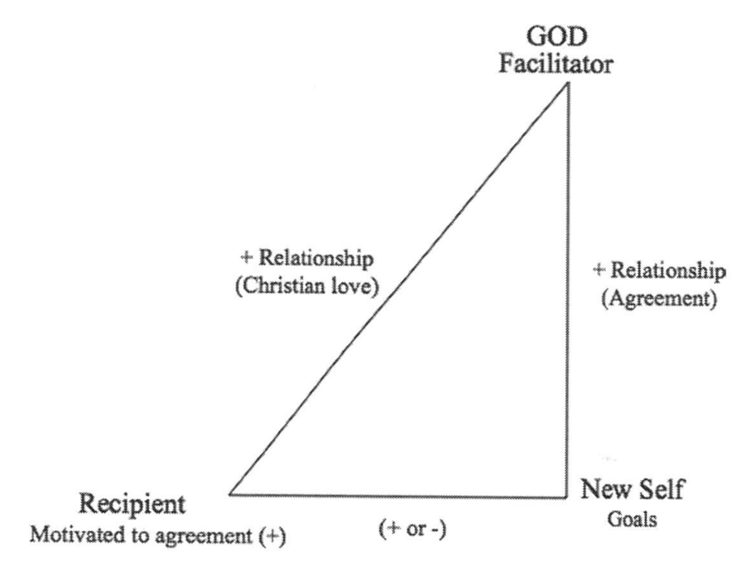

Figure 9-4

Resistance

Both the need to build a Christ-like relationship with the recipient and the need to communicate with the recipient that he or she will find hope in God's directives is imperative. The Apostles were commissioned to act as facilitators and proclaim the message of Christ to others. God gave them spiritual-attesting gifts that accredited both the messenger (love) and the message (hope) (see Acts 2:22 and Romans 15:18, 19) effectively creating two positive relationships. The secular counselor understands the necessity of building rapport with the client by demonstrating accurate empathic understanding, congruence and unconditional positive regard for the client. They also affirm their specific therapeutic goals of counseling through credentialing from their degrees, certifications, and experience. When a facilitator establishes two positive relationships, it creates a motivational environment that encourages the recipient to build a third positive relationship to maintain balance. When the situation arises wherein the recipient does not naturally build an affirmative relationship with the goals, the recipient is in a dissonant state and will begin to experience an uncomfortable level of anxiety. The recipient may accept this uncomfortable situation for a period of time, as he tries to resolve the conflict hindering him from relating appropriately with the goals. At some point, however, he will acknowledge that he is at an impasse and the discomfort created by the dissonant relationship triad will motivate him to attempt to regain balance by manipulating one of the other relationships.

As in our example with Carlos and Bethany, three obvious options are available to the recipient to alleviate the uncomfortable anxiety brought on by the dissonant relationships. The first option is to avoid the dissonant relationships all together. In this instance, the recipient seeks to end the personal relationship he has with the facilitator. He may simply get up and walk out of the room during a counseling session, or he may fail to show up for their next meeting. Secular counselors often refer to this client as a "no show," and wise counselors must reflect on the relationships in hope of identifying the dynamic that kept the recipient away. If the recipient chooses to continue in the relationship, he will focus his attention on the two other relationships in the triad. By changing one of the remaining positive relationships to a negative, he can regain balance. His first attack may focus on the relationship perceived to be the weakest. The strength of the facilitator-recipient relationship (love/rapport) will be viewed alongside the strength of the facilitator-goals relationship (hope/credentials). The weakest, most vulnerable relationship will likely then be manipulated. If he chooses to attack the facilitator-goals relationship, he will attempt to nullify the relationship by discrediting the message (goals) of the facilitator. He may offer up a challenge such as, "The

Bible was written two thousand years ago, and it is outdated and not relevant in today's world as a guide for modern man. Anyone who suggests that a person should think or act like they did two thousand years ago must be a religious nut." If such a reaction occurs in the secular counseling setting, "religious nut" is replaced with "quack." Think about it. By discrediting the message (goals), a recipient can regain balance and still maintain a decent relationship with the facilitator. Such people say things like, "Sure, so-and-so is a nice person, but her ideas are a little out there!"

A second option is to attack the facilitator-recipient relationship by attempting to change, if even for a short while, the positive relationship to a negative. The degree to which the recipient goes depends on the severity of the dissonance being experienced. He may simply begin to distance himself from the facilitator, or he may become overtly angry with the facilitator. This phenomenon is common in psychoanalysis wherein the psychoanalyst intentionally allows for a weak psychoanalyst-patient relationship to encourage negative transference. According to psychoanalytic theory, negative transference occurs when a patient transfers negative feelings associated with a person from his or her life through which some type of unconscious conflict had originated. The psychoanalyst believes that by interpreting the negative feelings, and identifying the individual those feelings should be directed toward, insight is gained into the conflict. I believe the evidence more strongly supports an attempt to regain balance.

To further support this, we will examine another facilitative relationship. If we consider the parent-child facilitative relationship, we discover that the same phenomena seen in counseling can be observed in this relationship. A parent's task is to "train up a child in the way he should go" (Proverbs 22:6). The parent instructs the child on how to think, how to talk, and how to act. If a child rejects this instruction, a dissonant relationship triad is experienced. The child can respond in a manner similar to the recipient in our counseling example. She may begin by attempting to avoid the dissonant relationships altogether. Depending on the level of dissonance experienced, her response could range from emotionally distancing herself from her parents all the way to the extreme of running away. If she chooses to attack the credibility of the parent, she will rationalize that the instruction does not apply to her because she lives in a world her parents cannot understand. She might say something like, "Mom, I love you, but you're still living in the eighties!" Call this tactic "the generation gap." Finally, if the credibility attack won't work and the child needs instant relief from the dissonant situation, she will simply say those three dreaded words, "I hate you!" Is this negative transference? I do not believe the evidence supports that hypothesis.

One final observation regarding dissonant relationships: If the recipient is experiencing dissonance in the relationship triad, the facilitator also may experience dissonance in the relationship triad. If the facilitator has established positive relationships with the recipient and the goals, but the recipient has resisted building a positive relationship with the goals, both the facilitator and the recipient will experience dissonance. Additionally, just as the recipient may attempt to regain balance by manipulating relationships, the facilitator may attempt to regain balance by manipulating the same relationships. If the facilitator manipulates his relationship with the recipient, he may begin to distance himself from the recipient or may even become angry. Of course, psychoanalysis would call this a form of "negative counter-transference." A more common approach for a counselor to regain balance occurs when the counselor affirms that the recipient is incapable of change and that he is a "lost cause." Of course, there are no "lost causes" in one-anothering, because it is God working through the Holy Spirit that redefines souls. Finally, a third option is available to secular counselors. They can simply change the goals to suit the client. This is not an option for those facilitating on Christ's behalf because the goals are firmly established in God and specified through His word.

As ambassadors for Christ, we are commanded to build an affirmative relationship with others and clearly establish that the goals of the facilitative relationship are grounded in God's Word. These two affirmative relationships have the potential for creating cognitive dissonance for the recipient. The question that begs for an answer is, "What should we do when a recipient is not building a faith relationship with the goals?" The first thing to consider is why a recipient is resistant to change. People fail to build a faith relationship with new-self goals for two reasons. The first reason is simple pride; they "don't want to," and, thus, admit a weakness they do not accept. We know that pride, or self-love, motivates people to live by sight, not by faith. The second reason people do not build a faith relationship with new-self goals is that they do not know how to build that relationship. Anyone who has raised children has experienced both these scenarios. There are times when a child finds trouble because he or she does not want to do the right thing. There are other times when a child finds trouble because he or she does not know how to do the right thing. In either case, we reflect on the steps of faith for guidance. As we consider the process of faith, we recall that it includes goodness, knowledge, self-control, and perseverance. The new-self goals of Christian one-anothering are discovered through God's Word (knowledge). Knowledge informs what to do, but the first step, goodness, creates the desire to do it. Jesus often concluded His teaching, wherein He was conveying the knowledge of God's will to the people, with the statement, "He who has ears, let him hear" (see Matthew 11:15 for one example). What Jesus was saying is that people with a humble attitude would hear His words and act on them. When we develop a healthy Christian attitude in our recipients, we are in essence developing their ears to hear. Only after we are assured that they have the proper attitude do we begin to search the Word of God for knowledge applicable to their specific issues. We continue walking alongside as they express their faith by guiding them into an understanding of how to put God's will for their lives into practice (self-control), and we continue with them when they stumble in order to pick them up and encourage them to stay committed (perseverance) to a life of faith. The best way to keep a negative faith relationship from causing problems in a facilitative relationship is to walk alongside the recipients, each step of the way, as they personally affirm that relationship.

Motivational Dynamics of One-Anothering

When a client enters into a relationship with a counselor, the client's soul or personhood is redefined to some extent, simply due to the new relationship. The change may be positive if the client focuses on the potential of the relationship to ease his burden in the present and to offer answers and hope for the future. Conversely, the change may be negative if the client believes the relationship signifies that he is incompetent to handle his own problems and a failure in some way. Regardless of the outcome, the human soul is defined by relationships, so any new relationship will redefine a soul in some way. One-anothering is a facilitative relationship in that it has a purpose or goal. The purpose or goal of a Christian one-anothering relationship is to facilitate the process of re-defining another's soul by bringing that soul into an appropriate relationship with the will of God. It is not the facilitative relationship itself that redefines a person to be what God wants. It is the relationship that fulfills the goal of a one-anothering relationship that redefines that person by God's standards. As such, the area of interest as we pursue motivational dynamics within the context of the seven soul-defining relationships will be on the goal relationship. More specifically, we will address the dynamics as they relate to bringing a person closer to the will of God.

When we enter into a facilitative relationship, we acknowledge all of the following truths. The recipient is experiencing despair, and consequently a motivating level of discomfort, because of some problem in his life. This discomfort exists because the recipient's thoughts, words, and deeds, as they relate to this issue, are apart from the will of God. If we can identify the problem thoughts, words, and deeds and bring them into the will of God, healing will take place. The problem may simply cease to exist. In other cases, the problem may still exist; however, the person will find peace and joy through Christ even in the midst of trials.

We have examined the motivational dynamics in the context of the one-anothering relationship triad. The next natural question is, "How do these motivational dynamics play out as we attempt to move a person out of the worldly triad and into the will of God?" We now expand our examination of motivational dynamics to all seven soul-defining relationships. We begin by noting that, according to the principles of cognitive consistency, the three relationships on the right side of the model are constants in that they are unchanging. (See figure 9-5.) God is always in agreement with His directives (new-self goals), so that relationship is always positive. Satan and the world are always in agreement, as they represent what is apart from God (old-self goals), so that relationship is always positive. Finally, God's will for our lives (new-self) and the world's directives for man (old-self) are always in disagreement, so the relationship between the two is always negative. So the relationships on the right side of the model remain the same. As we continue to explore these relationship triads, we see that a person whose thoughts, words, or deeds are not in line with the will of God will have a positive relationship with the world and the things of the world. He is motivated by self-love, enabled by some deception and empowered by the spirit of falsehood. So the worldly relationship triad (bottom triad in figure 9-5) is balanced with zero negative relationships (see 1 John 4:5). If the recipient has a positive, balanced relationship with the world, he must have a negative relationship with God and His directives.

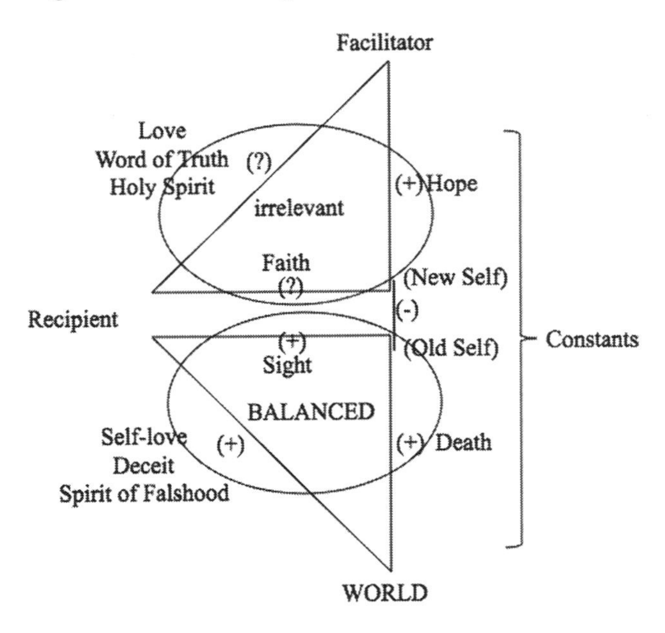

Recipient has been deceived and is living by sight.

Figure 9-5

A person can function in the worldly relationship triad without experiencing dissonance. It is only when hopelessness is inferred that he will experience despair, or a truth challenges the deception that he will experience dissonance.

If, after attempting to meet his needs in ways that do not fulfill, he infers the futility and hopelessness associated with living by sight, he will begin to fall into a state of despair. Despair is experienced when the deception that enabled his thoughts, words and deeds (living by sight) is exposed and he has exhausted his resources to meet his needs. (See figure 9-6.) He us unaware, for whatever reasons, of the hope offered by the spiritual triad and he has rejected the relationships in the worldly triad. The full rejection of the worldly relationship triad leads to the experience of the "depressive triad" discussed in chapter four. We also recall that a client enters into a counseling relationship because he is experiencing a motivating level of discomfort and he believes the counselor has built a relationship, either through academics or experience, with something that will offer him hope. When a person experiences this despair he is searching for, and is most receptive to, God's truth.

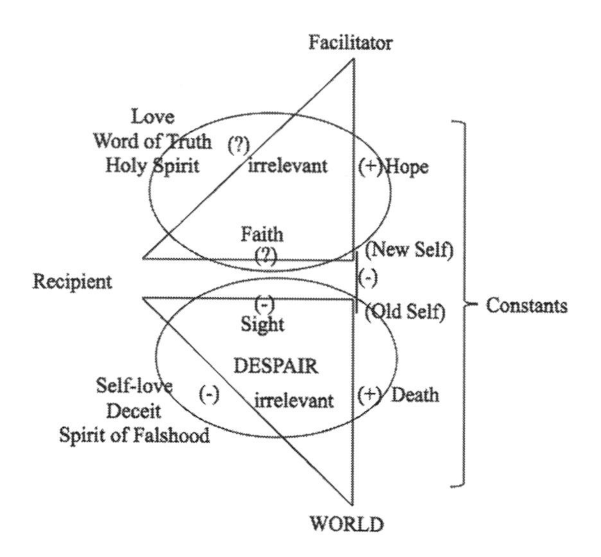

Recipient is in despair after inferring the hopeless associated with his lifestyle.

Figure 9-6

If truth challenges the deception, either by way of his own internal conscience or by way of an external facilitator, he will reject the deception and the resulting negative relationship with the world will create dissonance in both triads. He has rejected the deception offered by Satan and the world, however he is living by sight. He has accepted the truth of God, however he is not yet living by faith. (See figure 9-7.)

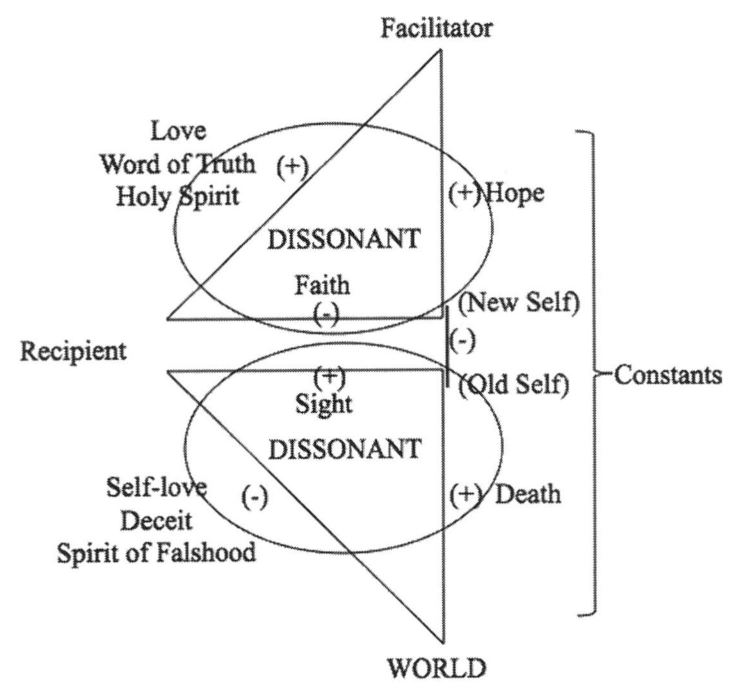

Figure 9-7

These two dissonant relationship triads will motivate him to reject his life of sin and begin living by faith, thereby balancing the spiritual relationship triad and relegating the worldly triad as irrelevant. (See figure 9-8.)

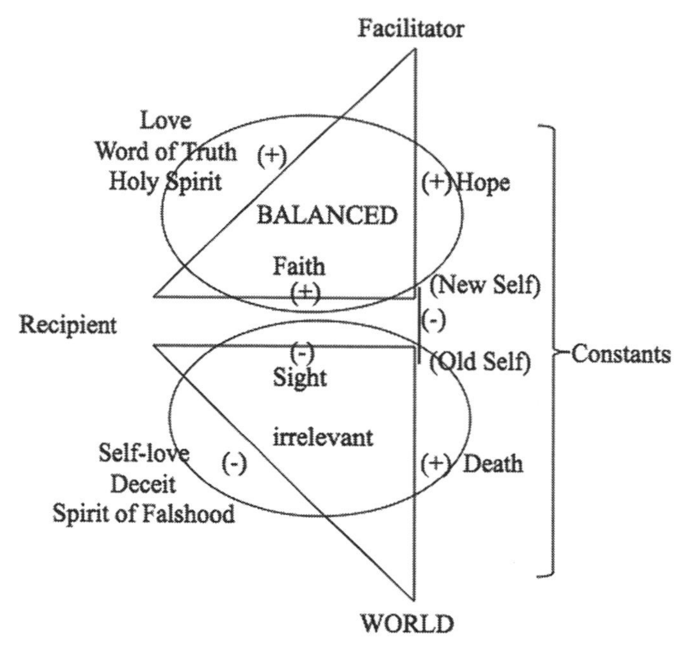

Figure 9-8

Since our focus is primarily on the latter situation that involves a facilitator, we will look at two examples from Scripture wherein truth was introduced in order to create dissonance and the potential to bring about change in the form of Christian maturity. First, in Luke 15, Jesus is the facilitator of change, and the "Pharisees and the teachers of the law" (verse 2) are the recipients. The Pharisees' and teachers' believed that Jesus should spend His time on earth with the righteous and not with people who were obviously sinners. Surely they did not associate with such people! As such, they were motivated by self-love and enabled by a deception that was testified to by the spirit of falsehood. In this case the spirit of falsehood probably presented itself as a need for affiliation with their peers, for there is both security and authority in numbers. Jesus desired to present a truth that could not coexist with the lie they believed. We recall that to whatever degree light is introduced, darkness is dispelled. He could have simply stated, as he did later, the He had come to "seek and to save what was lost" (Luke 19:10); however, here Jesus took a more indirect approach to communicate that truth in cumulative way. Jesus told them three parables to gradually develop a receptive attitude (goodness) in the hearers and allow them to infer the underlying truth (knowledge). He began with the parables of the lost sheep and the lost coin. Each parable conveyed to the recipients the joy of finding something that was lost, and Jesus made application after each parable to the saving of souls.

In the third parable, Jesus introduced a caricature that represented the Pharisees and the teachers of the law. This caricature was the brother of the lost son. We know that when the lost son returned, his father rejoiced, gave him gifts and celebrated. When the brother, who represented the Pharisees and teachers of the law, who had been faithful found out about the gifts and the celebration he became angry and refused to see his brother and celebrate his return. When the father approached his faithful son, the son specified the problem he was having. The faithful son said, "Look! All these years I've been slaving for you and never disobeyed your orders. Yet you never gave me even a young goat so I could celebrate with my friends. But when this son of yours who has squandered your property with prostitutes comes home, you kill the fattened calf for him" (verses 29, 30). The father then presented a truth that opposed the lie. The father replied, "My son, you are always with me, and everything I have is yours. But we had to celebrate and be glad, because this brother of yours was dead and is alive again; he was lost and is found" (verses 31, 32). Jesus ended the parable without telling the recipients if the brother changed his attitude and rejoiced over the finding of his brother or remained angry about his return. Jesus left the decisions to the hearers of the parables. Every parable Jesus told throughout the Gospels was to present a truth to oppose an obvious deception. Parables offered basics truths, in the context of everyday life lessons that were usually indirect enough to not be a threat to the hearer.

Our second example is more direct in nature. In 1 Corinthians 3, Paul is the writer of the epistle and the facilitator of the relationship. The recipients are the readers, the members of the church in Corinth. Paul is very direct in his relationship with the readers of the letter; likely because he believed his relationship with them was strong enough to withstand the direct approach. Paul tells them that they are "worldly" because there is "jealousy and quarreling" among them (verse 3). Paul makes the connection between the process and the product. Or, as Jesus said, "by their fruit you shall know them" (Matthew 7:20). Jealousy and quarreling are acts of the sinful nature produced when one walks by sight. Walking by sight is a process motivated by self-love, enabled by deception and empowered by the spirit of falsehood. The deception they had accepted was that they could raise their status in the local church by claiming they follow either Apollos or Paul. The resulting pride they felt was likely the sprit of falsehood that testified to the deception. Paul quickly presents a truth that cannot coexist with this deception when he states, "What, after all, is Apollos? And what is Paul? Only servants, through whom you came to believe—as the Lord has assigned to each his task. I planted the seed, Apollos watered it, but God made it grow" (verses 5, 6). In other words, one cannot raise his status by following field laborers - the lowest people in the hierarchy!

How a facilitator introduces truth will depend on the level of relationship that exists with the recipient. When I ponder relationship dynamics between the facilitator, the recipient, and the goals of the relationship, I recall an experience I had in graduate school. The class break was nearly over, and I was walking down the hallway toward our classroom when I heard a fellow student mention the name of a well-known Christian apologist. This immediately caught my attention, because the university I was attending and the Christian apologist seemed to have little in common. I noticed a group of classmates who obviously lived quite far from the will of God, examining a poster on the wall publicizing an upcoming lecture by this apologist on the university campus. The poster claimed that this individual was one of the most requested speakers on college and university campuses across the country and that he was booked for speaking engagements for many years to come. Nowhere on the poster did it state his expertise nor the topic he would be presenting. I acknowledged the potential and made a comment something like, "I read one of his books. I expect that it will be worth your while to attend." I quickly moved toward the classroom before anyone had time to ask for details. I took my seat in the classroom as the group that had been looking at the poster came in excitedly talking about the upcoming lecture. To my amazement one of the male students, one who was trying to set a record for living the furthest from God's will, announced to the whole class, "We're going to hear 'so and so' lecture on Friday evening. Everyone should come if they can." I thought about how the poster on the wall in the hallway had started the rapport building and credentialing with my fellow students. I then recalled the typical approach taken by this specific lecturer. He would come into the great hall and begin to build rapport with the university students as he conveyed his own university experience as an atheist. He would explain to them how, as a student, he set out to prove there was not a God. They would be smiling, cheering him on, and patting each other on the back for making the decision to come to the lecture. Very gradually he would begin to explain the spiritual transformation that took place in his life as he explored the Word of God in an attempt to prove it wrong. Finally, he would present a message of hope through Jesus Christ. Would they stay and listen to the whole message? I did not know. I did know that the apologist would do his best to give them ears to hear and that he was a competent ambassador for Christ and facilitator of His Truth. I also recall that I said a prayer.

CONCLUSION

We recall that one of the criticisms leveled against the development of a Christian psychology is that the Bible does not specifically address the counseling relationship. That is true, because the Bible is actually a guide for all Christian facilitative relationships of which counseling is only one. An understanding of the Biblical relationships provides direction for all one-anothering relationships. I'd like the reader to take a few minutes and think about the relationships in figure 10-1 from the perspective of facilitator. More specifically, think about the relationships from the facilitative one-anothering perspective you currently occupy. One reader might be pondering these relationships in the context of parenting, another in the context of ministry, and yet another in the context of counseling. Regardless of the specific role you play as facilitator, you should acknowledge a sense of clarity and guidance, as you have come to understand how you are to function, as an ambassador for Christ, within the context of the relationships that potentially define the soul of another. You have a deeper appreciation of the motivational and relational properties of Christian love. You understand that you cannot force a person to live by faith; however, they can be motivated by love and inspired by hope. As you communicate the love of Christ to others, and the hope that comes from living in His will, you begin to develop a proper attitude in the recipient (goodness). You realize that the word of God is the sole measure of man and that which enables one's faith. Consequently, you hold the recipients thoughts, words and deeds along side God's word to identify ways in which he has deviated from the will of God. You rely on the guidance provided by God and communicate His truth to others to accurately meet their needs. In humility, you acknowledge you are a field laborer in all you do and it is God who makes things grow. Therefore, you rely on the work of the Holy Spirit as He works in your life and the lives of others to bring about Christian maturity. You help the recipient engage his mind in Christian reasoning as you search to determine the correct path to take by applying biblical principles to the problem at hand. You then walk with the recipient as they implement these new thoughts, words and deeds. Regardless of the specific type of facilitation you are engaged in, you will experience clarity and direction given this more thorough understanding of God's will as you one-another on His behalf. You will also experience clarity and understanding as you ponder what it is to be a recipient in this relationship where God is the facilitator. We never want to loose the joy of knowing we are in Christ Jesus and the burden of sharing that joy with those who are searching. We all have a testimony: We were lost and now are found.

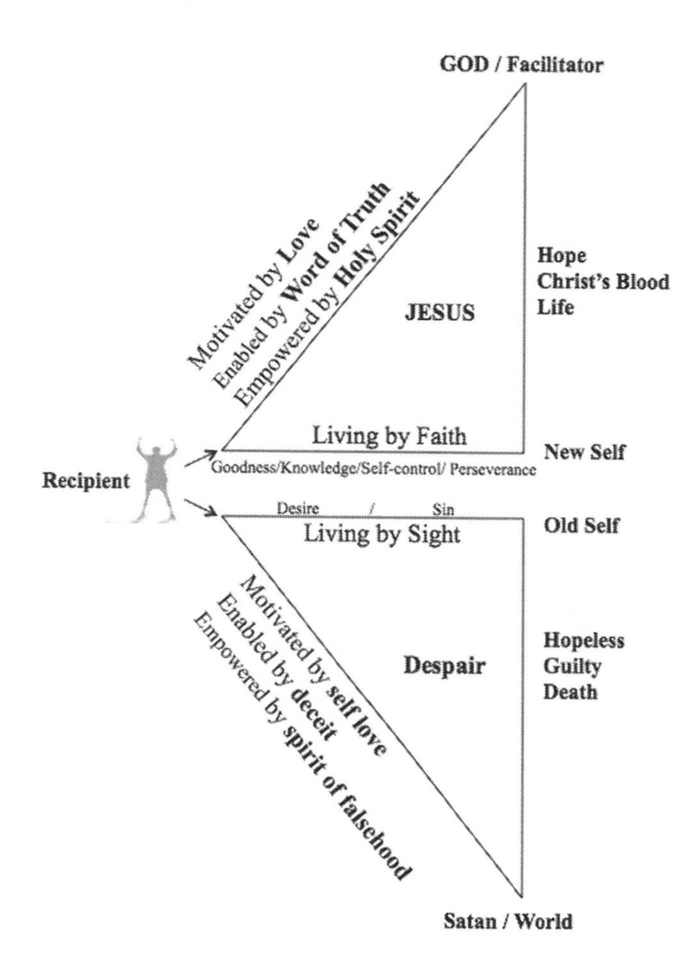

Figure 10-1

Reference List

Abelson, R. P., Aronson, W. J., Newcomb, T. M., & Rosenberg, P. H. (1974). *Theories of cognitive consistency: A source book.* Rand McNally.

Aristotle. *Magna moralia.* 1 (35), 1197.

Beck, A. T. (1979). *Cognitive therapy of depression.* New York: Guilford.

Benner D.G. (Ed.). (1999). *Baker encyclopedia of psychology & counseling (2nd ed.).* Grand Rapids, MI: Baker Books.

Boneau, C. A. (1998). *Herman Ebbinghaus: On the road to progress or down the garden path?*: Vol. 3. *Portraits of Pioneers in Psychology.* Mahwah, NJ: Lawrence Erlbaum.

Brown, C, (Ed.). (1986). *New international dictionary of New Testament theology (4 vols.).* Grand Rapids, MI: Zondervan.

Calvin, J. (1559). *Institutes of the Christian religion.* Westminster John Knox Press, translation edition (January 1, 1960).

Chambless, D. L. (1993). *Task force on promotion and dissemination of psychological procedures: a report adopted by the division 12 board. American Psychological Association.* Retrieved from http://www.apa.org/divisions/div12/est/chamble2.pdf

Cottrell, J. (2002). *The faith once for all.* Joplin, MO: College Press Publishing Company.

Ebbinghaus, H. (1885/1962). *Memory: a contribution to experimental psychology*. New York: Dover.

Festinger, L. (1957). *A theory of cognitive dissonance*. Palo Alto, CA: Stanford University Press.

Heider, F. (1958). *The psychology of interpersonal relationships.* New York: Wiley.

Hodge, C. (2003). *Systematic Theology (vol. 2)*. Hendrickson Publishers.

Kierkegaard, S. (1941). *A sickness unto death.* Princeton, NJ: The Princeton University Press.

Jeeves, M. (2002). *Changing portraits of human nature. Science and Christian belief,* 14(1).

Johnson, E. (2004). *Locating Christian psychology. Edification: The newsletter of the Society for Christian Psychology,* 1(2), 13-14.

Johnson, E. (2004). *Edification: The newsletter of the Society for Christian Psychology,* 1(3), 1.

Jost, G. (1897). *Die associationsfestigkeit in iher abhangigkeit von der verteilung der wierderholungen. Zeitschriftfur psychologie,* 14, 436-472.

Kidwell, R. J. (1977). *Ecclesiastes.* Joplin, MO: College Press.

Kirwan, W. T. (1984). *Biblical concepts for Christian counseling: a case for integrating psychology and theology.* Grand Rapids, MI: Baker Academic.

Lewis, C. S. (1952). *Mere Christianity.* New York: MacMillan Publishing Company.

McFall, R. M. (1991). *Manifesto for a science of clinical psychology. The clinical psychologist,* 44(6), 75-88.

Neander, A. (1853). *The relation of the Grecian to Christian ethics. Bibliotheca Sacra,* 10, 810.

Plantinga, A. (1993). *Warrant and proper function.* New York: Oxford University Press.

Plantinga, A. (2000). *Warranted Christian belief.* New York: Oxford University Press.

Richards, L. R. (1999). *Spirit. New international encyclopedia of bible words.* Grand Rapids, MI: Zondervan Publishing House.

Roberts, R. C., & Talbot, M. R. (1997). *Limning the psyche: explorations in Christian psychology.* William B. Eerdmans Publishing Company.

Roberts, R. C. (2003). *Edification: the newsletter of the Society for Christian Psychology,* 1(1), 1.

Silverman, L. H., & Weinberger J. (1985). *Mommy and I are one. American Psychologist,* 40(12), 192.

Woody, S. R., Weisz, J., & McLean, C. (2005). *Empirically supported treatments: 10 years later. The Clinical Psychologist,* 58(4), 5-11.

Made in the USA
Charleston, SC
23 December 2012